Honey and maple syrup might be better for you than sugar. They might be better for the environment. But even better, and sweet as anything, is how these natural ingredients taste and the wonders they do for a dish. James Beard Award–winning cookbook author **Beth Dooley** and gifted photographer **Mette Nielsen** make the most of these flavors in this celebration of honey and maple syrup in traditional kitchens as well as cutting-edge food culture.

Full of easy ideas that include honey and maple syrup in foods both savory and sweet, this book features a wide range of irresistible recipes for breakfast, lunch, and dinner, for snacks and salads, condiments and vegetables, entrées and desserts, syrups, cocktails, and elixirs. Sweeten your table with rosemary honey butter, green tomato chutney, curry marinated herring, brown butter honey popcorn, savory maple black pepper biscotti, oven-roasted chicken thighs with pomegranate molasses, honey-glazed salmon salad, maple vanilla half-pound cake, elderberry throat coat, bourbon maple smash, and more.

With its innovative recipes, practical tips, conversion charts, historical and scientific facts, nutritional value information, suggestions for storage and sourcing, and above all Mette Nielsen's remarkable photographs, *Sweet Nature* invites us to fully enjoy these two iconic ingredients from nature's pantry.

SWEET NATURE

ALSO PUBLISHED BY THE UNIVERSITY OF MINNESOTA PRESS

Savory Sweet: Simple Preserves from a Northern Kitchen
Beth Dooley and Mette Nielsen

The Birchwood Cafe Cookbook
Tracy Singleton and Marshall Paulson with Beth Dooley
Photography by Mette Nielsen

Minnesota's Bounty: The Farmers Market Cookbook
Beth Dooley

The Sioux Chef's Indigenous Kitchen
Sean Sherman with Beth Dooley

The Northern Heartland Kitchen
Beth Dooley

Savoring the Seasons of the Northern Heartland
Beth Dooley and Lucia Watson

SWEET
NATURE

a cook's guide
to using honey and
maple syrup

beth dooley & mette nielsen
food styling by abby wyckoff

University of Minnesota Press
Minneapolis · London

The authors extend special gratitude to Abby Wyckoff for her excellent food styling for this book.

Photographs on pages 3 and 9 courtesy Shutterstock.com. All other photographs by Mette Nielsen.

Published by the University of Minnesota Press
111 Third Avenue South, Suite 290
Minneapolis, MN 55401-2520
http://www.upress.umn.edu

Book design by Brian Donahue and Jessica Collette / bedesign, inc.
Photographs prepared for printing by color specialist Timothy Meegan

Printed in Canada on acid-free paper

The University of Minnesota is an equal-opportunity educator and employer.

24 23 22 21 20 19   10 9 8 7 6 5 4 3 2 1

Library of Congress Cataloging-in-Publication Data
Dooley, Beth, author. | Nielsen, Mette, author.
Sweet Nature : a cook's guide to using honey and maple syrup / Beth
    Dooley and Mette Nielsen ; food styling by Abby Wyckoff.
Minneapolis : University of Minnesota Press, [2019] | Includes
    bibliographical references and index.
Identifiers: LCCN 2018037436 | ISBN 978-1-5179-0470-8 (hc)
Subjects: LCSH: Cooking (Honey) | Cooking (Maple sugar and syrup) | LCGFT:
    Cookbooks.
Classification: LCC TX767.H7 D66 2019 | DDC 641.6/8—dc23
LC record available at https://lccn.loc.gov/2018037436

To Kevin, Matt, Kip, and Tim,
for our sweet life!

—BETH

To Alexander and Abby,
for our shared love of gardening,
cooking, and eating!

—METTE

CONTENTS

INTRODUCTION

Maple syrup and honey are as good for us as they are for the land, water, and air, and are better-tasting, healthy, and versatile alternatives to refined sugar. As we all seek to source real, unprocessed foods, locally sourced and sustainably produced honey and maple syrup are reliable staples in every good cook's pantry.

Rich in story and lore, both maple syrup and honey have delighted cooks through the ages, and today they are among the key ingredients in a vibrant local food system and economy. Maple trees, with their broad leafy canopies, shelter birds and small wildlife, retain groundwater, capture carbon, prevent erosion, and return nutrients to the soil. Honeybees are prodigious pollinators of flowers, fruits, vegetables, trees, and berry and nut bushes, and are necessary to every garden and farm. Especially in the Northern Heartland region, the sustainable harvest of these important foods provides a reliable income stream for area farmers. The glorious maple, burnishing our hillsides yellow in autumn and shimmering green come summer, defines our seasons. Those blooming flowers that feed the bees grace our prairies and yards. Who can deny the importance of the beauty such foods add to our landscape? Here are nature's unrequited gifts, a source of pleasure, sustenance, and joy.

Maple syrup is the flavor of memory shared by those who live in Minnesota, Wisconsin, Iowa, and Illinois and enjoy local syrup that is uniquely smooth and silky with distinctive hints of caramel and toffee. It is the only indigenous sweetener, delighting the earliest people whose ancient techniques play out in kitchens today. It is the foundation for healing tonics and potions, marinades, bastes, and sauces (savory and sweet), and it is a preservative with uses that extend beyond pancakes. Human use of honey dates back as far as 7000 BC, depicted in cave paintings found in Spain. Prior to European colonization, indigenous people in North America gathered honey from wild bees before beekeeping was introduced in the 1600s. Honey's viscous texture and nuanced favors reflect the flowers bees feast on, yielding a sweet taste of place.

Nature's sweet gifts offer a range of possibilities in the kitchen, and maple syrup and honey enhance a wide variety of savory dishes, beverages, preserves, and blissful desserts. Here are our best recipes, kitchen tips and hints, and stories that celebrate this bounty. Forget the white stuff—honey and maple are oh so good.

MAPLE SYRUP

Maple sap is the surest sign of spring and, once simmered into syrup, the first local food to appear in our Northern Heartland. As the days lengthen and the snows melt, the sap begins to run. Throughout our forests, the scent of sap simmering in kettles over an open fire announces the promise of warmer days to come. Maple syrup will vary from season to season, from forest to forest, from tree to tree. No batch of maple syrup is the same—each tastes of the frigid winter, crusty spring snow, the brightening light, the damp forest floor, of our weather, water, soil, and the legacies of the people who "sugared" before us.

The Ojibwe refer to the maple tree as *aninaatig* and their methods for tapping these trees rely on close attention to and understanding of the forests. To this day, many Native communities celebrate the *Iskigamizige-Giizis* ("Maple Sugar Moon"), usually the first full moon of April or May, with ceremonies of thanksgiving and feasts. According to tradition, when the eagles return, the sap begins to flow, the sign for the tribes to move from their winter lodges to establish sugar camps in the maple groves. Years ago, they used spouts carved from cedar and collected the sap in birch-bark containers sealed with pine pitch and then boiled the sap into syrup or sugar in clay pots heated with rocks pulled from the fire. When cooked all the way down to evaporate all the liquid, the syrup became sugar. It was then molded into blocks that were far easier to transport than liquid syrup.

Sap was often left out to ferment into "sour sap." Quite like vinegar, sour sap was used to baste roasting meats and to brighten simmering stews. Maple syrup has been an ingredient in a variety of traditional medicines—pounded with bark for a poultice to treat wounds, simmered with herbs to soothe sore throats. Chunks of maple sugar, carried by hunters and warriors, provided quick energy.

Several species of maple trees yield sap, but the sugar maple is the most productive source. These magnificent trees can grow as tall as ninety feet with canopies, or crowns, spreading up to eighty feet wide. Many of these trees date back to the mid-1800s. Like oak and willow, maple trees are deciduous and release their leaves each autumn, producing "samaras," winged papery seeds (whirligigs) that are carried on the wind to fertile ground.

Maple trees grow together in clusters called a sugar bush and require a diverse environment to be healthy, including a variety of different trees, dense forest undergrowth, birds, and small wildlife. In the heat of spring, the maple tree begins brewing sap. Water moves from the roots up to the tree's branches and out to the leaves for photosynthesis, a process that adds sugar and energy to the liquid and creates the sweet sap. The more leaves, the more sugar the tree will produce.

Maple trees need the cold nights and warm days of late March through late April for the sap to run. During the day, the starch stored in the trees' roots for winter rises up through the trunk and is trapped as sap. At night, when the temperatures drop, the sap stops but flows again in the warmth of the day. The interior of the tree functions like a giant pump that, as the season progresses, pushes the sap out of the tree. A mere 10 percent of the tree's sap is removed during the sugaring season, so the tree still receives its necessary water and nutrients as it is being tapped. A tree needs around forty years and to grow to twelve inches in diameter to become mature enough to produce sap, and healthy trees will then produce sap for syrup throughout their lives.

Mette and I have helped harvest maple syrup at a friend's cabin in northern Wisconsin using these old-fashioned methods. We drilled a small hole into the tree trunk, inserted a short, hollow metal tube (called a *spile*), where the bucket is hung to collect the sap.

Once the clear, mildly sweet liquid was retrieved from the trees, we schlepped it through the snow to an outdoor cauldron set over a roaring wood fire where the sap was boiling down into syrup. This process created a tremendous amount of steam and transformed what was initially 2 percent sugar in the sap into the 66 percent sugar for thick syrup (it takes about thirty to forty gallons of sap to make one gallon of syrup). As the sap became sweeter and more concentrated, we took turns, stirring through the night, watching to be sure it didn't burn, sipping whiskey-spiked maple tea, coffee, and maple cocoa. Toward the end, we drizzled syrup in the snow, where it hardened into maple candy.

These days in the larger commercial operations, the trees are tapped with bright blue plastic tubes that pipe sap into an enclosed sugar shack where the syrup is boiled down using automated evaporators and machinery that filters and bottles the syrup. The process of simmering sap into maple syrup and then into maple sugar hasn't changed much from the early days: maple sugar is simply what remains after all the liquid from the syrup has been evaporated. Maple sugar is perhaps the easiest to substitute for processed sugar in baking, as the ratio is one to one. It stores indefinitely and adds a deeper, more distinct flavor to foods.

MAPLE SYRUP IN THE KITCHEN

Maple syrup and maple sugar are rich tasting and complex, with far more flavor than processed sugar. Unlike processed sugar, maple syrup and maple sugar are full of antioxidants, vitamins, and minerals, have lower scores on the glycemic index, and help fight inflammatory diseases and prevent cancer. Maple syrup and maple sugar are also easy to digest.

In 2014, the U.S. Department of Agriculture (USDA) and Canada revised maple syrup standards into grades in order to simplify and define the differences in syrups collected and simmered during different times of the season. All syrups are now graded A with descriptors; the use of B as a grade has been discontinued.

Grade A: Golden Color and Delicate Flavor
This is the first syrup made from sap that runs in March. It has the lightest color and most delicate flavor, and it is best for traditional uses where its mild taste shines through: pancakes, waffles, oatmeal, and yogurt.

Grade A: Amber Color and Rich Flavor
A little darker, this grade of syrup is created from midseason sap and has a smoother, rounder flavor. It's good for baking and great in cocktails and tea.

Grade A: Darker Color and Robust Flavor
Darker, stronger, and deeper, with overtones of brown sugar, this syrup is terrific in a barbecue sauce and as a glaze for grilled meat. Try it in coffee or as an unconventional pairing for mild cheese.

Grade A: Very Dark and Strong Flavor
This is the most robust, maple-packed maple syrup from the season's last sap. Strong tasting and thick, it's a delicious alternative to molasses in baked goods.

BAKING WITH MAPLE SYRUP AND MAPLE SUGAR

Substitute maple syrup for refined sugar with these modifications:

- For every 1 cup of processed sugar, substitute ⅔ cup of maple syrup.

- Reduce the quantity of liquid ingredients in a recipe (water, milk, juice) by about ¼ cup.

- Keep in mind the different flavors of each grade of maple syrup. The stronger, bolder syrups will impart more distinct maple tones, so choose recipes for these syrups in which the maple will not compete with or overwhelm the taste of the other ingredients. It's best to taste syrups first before using.

- Lower the temperature when baking with maple syrup by 25°F.

- Maple syrup can serve as a one-to-one substitute for liquid sweeteners such as molasses, agave, and corn syrup.

Substitute maple sugar for refined sugar with these modifications:

- Substitute one to one for processed sugar in any recipe. The maple flavor (and texture) will vary depending on where it was produced.

- If the sugar appears to be coarse, grind it first in a coffee mill, spice grinder, or food processor fitted with a steel blade.

- Choose recipes so that the other ingredients do not fight with or overwhelm the flavor of the maple sugar. Taste before using maple sugar.

Another maple substitute we love is maple vinegar, which is fermented from maple sap before it is simmered into syrup. Its flavor is very close to mild apple cider vinegar, and we use it in recipes calling for apple cider vinegar whenever we can. It is not readily available and may be found online.

STORING MAPLE SYRUP

Once a container of maple syrup is opened, store it in a covered container in the refrigerator. If not properly stored, it may develop mold on the surface. If this happens, scoop off the mold and then bring the maple syrup to a boil. Cool, turn it into a glass container, and store in the refrigerator.

HONEY

Honeybees arrived in North America from Europe in the mid-1600s along with apple and plum trees planted by settlers in Jamestown, Virginia. Native Americans dubbed honeybees "White Man's Fly," for they had been collecting honey from the nests of wild bees, using smoke to confuse them before cracking open their hives. Within the century, indigenous people, too, began practicing the art of beekeeping.

In the mid-1800s, the "bee box" with removable wooden frames revolutionized beekeeping. It mimics the shallow chambers of a hive and allows beekeepers to collect honey without destroying the hive. Still popular today, the bee box makes it possible for farmers to pollinate different crops by moving it from field to field. This system of moving bees is especially critical to pollinating cranberry bogs. Honey farmers rely on bee boxes to collect and harvest single-source honey derived from single fields of clover, basswood, buckwheat, and so on.

Honey—pure, simple, concentrated nectar—is imbued with the sweetest associations of summer days, warm grasses, bees buzzing between flowers. Honey is food for the bees, the source of carbohydrates that gives them energy to fly, collect more nectar, and then make more honey. Bees collect the sticky nectar during the long, warm months to store in combs as food through the winter. Throughout the

world, honey is central to ceremonies and celebrations. The ancient Greeks gifted honey to the gods and to departed spirits as sacrificial offerings. It is customary on Rosh Hashanah, the Jewish New Year, to dip apples in honey to usher in a sweet new year. Honey is a component in Chinese wedding ceremonies, and small gifts of honey are often given to wedding guests as favors. Fermented honey (mead) was an intoxicant long before grapes were pressed into wine. Wax from the comb became candles for light.

The upper Midwest is the highest honey-producing region in the United States, yet yields are declining as crops of corn and soybeans replace flowering plants. The farm chemicals used to grow these monocrops have an immeasurable negative impact on bees' health.

Bees (aka angels of agriculture) are critical to our food supply. More than one-third of the world's crops, such as alfalfa seed, sunflowers, fruits, and vegetables, depend on bee pollination, an ecological service valued in North America at twenty billion dollars each year.

Our bees are endangered: managed hives have decreased by 50 percent since the 1950s as the amount of soy and corn acreage has expanded, fence row to fence row. The most nutritious and interesting components in our diets (fruits, vegetables, alfalfa for meat and dairy) are affected by the decline in bees.

The best way to support bees is through providing them with plenty of food: bees are all about pollen, and bee-friendly plants are easy to grow. Bees are especially drawn to blue, purple, and yellow flowers (clover is a great choice and an easy ground cover), and bees favor sage, salvia, oregano, lavender, ironweed, yarrow, hyssop, alfalfa, Echinacea, bee balm (of course), buttercup, goldenrod, and English thyme. You can find a complete list of bees' favorite plants on the University of Minnesota's Bee Lab website, https://www.beelab.umn.edu.

Beekeeping, both as a hobby and as a profession, is contributing to the health of our bees. As a local business, it contributes to the local economy. So, why resist this naturally sweet treat? It's just so good.

RAW HONEY

Raw honey is collected directly from an extractor that removes the honey through centrifugal force: a drum holds a frame basket that spins, flinging the honey out. At the Beez Kneez Honey House in Minneapolis, amateur beekeepers are invited to use the company's bicycle extractor for Pedal Powered Honey.

Raw honey is never heated or pasteurized, so it is the honey highest in nutritional value. Commercial honey has been pasteurized (heated to 70 degrees), then cooled for easy filtering and bottling—meant to make the honey look cleaner and more appealing on the shelf. Pasteurization prevents honey from fermenting and slows crystallization, but crystallization should not be a factor when considering the quality of the honey.

When raw honey is heated in baking or cooking, it loses its delicate aromas and flavor as well as the enzymes responsible for vitamins and minerals. In the recipes that do not require cooking, we call for raw honey. It is more expensive than processed honey, so you may choose to use commercial honey in baking and cooking recipes, where the honey is exposed to high temperatures.

SINGLE-SOURCE HONEY

When bees feast on a particular flower, the honey will reflect the flavor of the nectar as a "single-source" honey. Single-source honey is raw honey, not heated or processed, and differs from commercially produced honey, which is blended from different sources for overall consistency and pasteurized. Many beekeepers offer single-source honey that is identified by the flower that defines the flavor, ranging from the delicate basswood to the dark, strong buckwheat. To appreciate the distinct flavor of different single-source honeys, serve these unadorned with cheeses or drizzled on scones or toast.

Not all raw local honey is single source: some is collected from fields and forests with diverse plants. These honeys also reflect the plants that have fed these bees.

Here's a guide to the most common varieties of single-source honey in this vast, diverse Midwestern region. The name of the honey will be printed on the label with descriptions of flavor.

Alfalfa honey is a lovely, pale honey with subtle vanilla flavors.

Basswood, or linden flower, is the signature honey of this region, with wonderful, light floral notes. This delicate honey is best saved for drizzling over mild cheeses, toast, and scones, allowing its subtle flavor to shine through.

Buckthorn honey is the happy gift of this invasive plant. It's a lovely deep yellow honey with a nutty body and tangy finish.

Buckwheat honey's flavor is bold and distinct with hints of plum, cherry, and a slight bitterness reminiscent of molasses. Its strong flavor pairs nicely with goat or blue cheese.

Dandelion honey is the first honey produced by bees early in the season. Bright yellow like a dandelion flower, it has a distinctly sharp flavor with grapefruit overtones.

Dutch Clover honey comes from the clovers you see along roadsides and in meadows. Semisweet with a mild caramel flavor, it's a perfect all-purpose honey.

Fall Wildflower honey is the last honey produced each year, a deep amber color, reflecting the goldenrod and wetland flowers the bees feast on. It's herbal and grapey.

Honeydew honey, aka "forest honey," is very rare. Dark and thick, it has a high mineral content and a woodsy, malty flavor.

Locust honey is very light, with a floral, fruity, delicate flavor. You'll want to save this for foods that do not overwhelm its taste.

Purple Loostrife honey is one sweet offering of this invasive species with its toffee and fennel aromas and mild taste.

Savory Marsh Flower honey is a late-season honey collected from the flowers that grow near the marshy banks of the Mississippi River. Its nutty flavor makes it a fine match for cookies and cakes.

Sweet Clover is an all-around lovely honey with butter texture and light herbal notes. It is great with baked apples.

COOKING AND BAKING WITH HONEY

Honey is sweeter than sugar, so, when working with honey, make these modifications:

- For every 1 cup of sugar, substitute ½ to ⅔ cup honey.

- Reduce the total amount of liquids in the recipe: for every 1 cup of honey, subtract ¼ cup of the other liquids from the recipe.

- To balance the natural acids in the honey, add a little extra baking soda to baked-good recipes to help them rise properly: increase the amount of baking soda by ⅛ teaspoon for every cup of honey.

- The higher sugar content in honey helps baked foods caramelize and thus burn faster than with granulated sugar. Lower the heat and keep a watchful eye to avoid overbaking and burning.

- When measuring honey, lightly wipe the measuring spoon or cup with butter or oil, and the honey will slide right off.

- The nuanced aromas and tastes of delicate single-source or varietal raw honey are often lost when it is heated. The delicate flavor of these honeys may be overwhelmed when combined with strong flavors such as hot pepper, curry, and savory herbs.

STORING HONEY

Store honey at room temperature, away from direct sunlight. Don't refrigerate it; cold temperatures cause the honey to crystallize. If the honey does crystallize, place the jar in a pan of warm water and move it around until the crystals dissolve.

1

SWEET STARTS

Given the hectic nature of our mornings, it's tempting to skip breakfast and reach for a sugary treat on the run. But studies confirm that eating breakfast improves memory, focus, and attention: it's the most important meal of the day. These healthful breakfast dishes, packed with whole grains, nuts, and dried fruit, double as snacks for that afternoon slump; others can be prepared in the evening so they are ready to go when you are. Honey (with its enzymes, minerals, vitamins, and amino acids) and maple (full of antioxidants, vitamins, and minerals) give these recipes a sweet, healthful boost. And we don't skimp on indulgences . . . honey buns and maple bacon, why not! We added a few indulgences for a lazy weekend brunch. Sun's up—have a sweet day!

Honey-toasted Muesli with
Millet, with Simple Honey
Lime and Berry Sauce

HONEY-TOASTED MUESLI WITH MILLET

Makes about 6 cups

Wonderful with fresh fruit, crumbled onto yogurt, or added to trail mix for a satisfying snack. This will keep several weeks in a covered container.

1½ cups thick rolled oats or regular rolled oats

1 cup millet

1 cup hazelnuts, coarsely chopped

½ cup unsweetened coconut flakes

½ cup honey

½ cup chopped dates or other dried fruit

Preheat the oven to 350°F. Line a large baking sheet with parchment paper. Combine the oats, millet, chopped hazelnuts, coconut flakes, and honey in a large bowl and mix well so the honey coats the rest of the ingredients.

Spread in an even layer on the parchment-lined baking sheet and place on the middle rack of the oven. Bake until golden brown, about 20 minutes; rotate the pan front to back halfway through for more even toasting.

Remove from the oven and toss in the chopped dates; mix well. Cool completely on the pan before storing in an airtight container.

SWEET TIP: A light clover honey is terrific for this recipe.

NORTH COUNTRY MAPLE GRANOLA

Makes about 7 cups

Light and crunchy, not too sweet, this is our favorite granola for topping yogurt or snacking right out of hand. Try it layered with fruit and whipped cream for an easy dessert. We like unsweetened organic puffed rice, but any puffed rice works well. Vary the nuts and dried fruit as you please. This will store nicely in a covered container for several months.

---

3   **cups thick rolled oats**

1   **cup unsweetened puffed rice cereal**

1   **cup millet**

1   **cup coarsely chopped hazelnuts**

¼   **cup sunflower or vegetable oil**

¼   **cup maple syrup**

¼   **cup maple sugar**

½   **teaspoon sea salt**

1   **cup dried cranberries**

Preheat the oven to 350°F. In a large bowl, mix together all the ingredients except the dried cranberries, making sure ingredients are well coated with oil and maple syrup. Transfer the mixture to a large (13 x 18-inch) rimmed baking sheet lined with parchment paper and spread it out to an even layer.

Place in the middle of the oven and bake until golden brown, about 35 to 45 minutes, stirring and rotating the pan a couple of times.

Remove from the oven and stir in dried cranberries. Allow granola to cool completely on baking sheet before storing in an airtight container.

SWEET TIP: The dried cranberries that are sweetened with apple juice are less sweet than most commercial varieties.

BREAKFAST BREAD PUDDING

Serves 4

Prepare this the night before, to bake in the morning. It puts those odds and ends of good bread to good use. For a weekend treat, use rich challah or raisin bread.

- 3 tablespoons unsalted butter, melted
- 1½ generous cups bread cubes
- ¼ cup honey
  Generous pinch of salt
- 2 eggs, lightly beaten
- 1 teaspoon vanilla
- 2 teaspoons cinnamon
  Pinch of freshly grated nutmeg
- 1½ cups milk, heated to a boil
  Honey for drizzling (optional)

Preheat the oven to 350°F. Use about 1 tablespoon of the butter to grease a baking dish. Turn the bread cubes into the baking dish.

In a medium bowl, whisk together the honey, remaining butter, salt, eggs, vanilla, cinnamon, and nutmeg. Slowly whisk the milk into the honey mixture. Pour this evenly over bread cubes. Place the baking dish inside a larger dish and place into the oven. Carefully pour water into the outer dish until it's one inch deep.

Bake at 350°F until the pudding is just set and a knife inserted into the center comes out clean, about 35 to 40 minutes. Drizzle with a little honey and serve warm.

SWEET TIP: Slice leftover pudding into rectangles; panfry the cut sides in butter and serve topped with fresh fruit.

Honey Goodness

Raw honey contains antioxidants, helps reduce digestive disorders, and has a number of antibacterial properties. It's known to heal wounds and ease sores. It helps athletes recover after strenuous workouts faster than other sweeteners do. Honey's benefits may be damaged when exposed to high heat, so save the raw honey for sweetening tea, drizzling over oatmeal or yogurt, and garnishing baked foods such as the Breakfast Bread Pudding.

CRANAPPLE BAKED OATMEAL

Serves 6 to 8

Be sure to use old-fashioned rolled oats, not instant oats. To save time in the morning, assemble this dish the night before, store in the refrigerator, then bake it off as you're getting ready to go.

3 tablespoons unsalted butter, melted

2 cups rolled oats

½ cup toasted chopped walnuts or pecans

1 teaspoon baking powder

2 teaspoons cinnamon
Generous pinch of salt

⅓ cup maple syrup or honey

2 cups whole milk

1 large egg

2 teaspoons vanilla extract

1 large tart apple, such as Haralson, peeled, cored, and diced

1½ cups fresh blueberries
Additional maple syrup for drizzling and garnish

Preheat the oven to 375°F. Grease an 8-inch baking dish with 1 tablespoon of the butter.

In a medium bowl, mix together oats, nuts, baking powder, cinnamon, and salt.

In a separate bowl, whisk together honey, milk, egg, the remaining butter, and vanilla.

Arrange the apple pieces in the bottom of the prepared dish. Top with most of the berries. Cover fruit with the oat mixture, then slowly drizzle the milk mixture over the oats. Scatter the remaining berries over the top.

Bake the oatmeal until the top is golden and the oats are set, about 35 to 45 minutes. Remove and drizzle additional maple syrup over the top.

SWEET TIP: To toast nuts, scatter the nuts on a roasting pan and toast in a 350°F oven until you smell a toasty aroma when the nuts are nicely browned and crisp, about 3 to 8 minutes.

SUNFLOWER BRAN MUFFINS

Makes 12 muffins

Here's a better bran muffin. Not too sweet, and it's chock-full of plenty of bran so it's hearty and flavorful. Dried cranberries add pops of flavor to the warm spices. Thanks to the buttermilk, this muffin stays moist and has a very tender crumb, while sunflower seeds add a nice nutty crunch.

1⅓ cups all-purpose flour

1⅓ cups wheat bran

1¼ teaspoons baking powder

½ teaspoon baking soda

2 teaspoons cinnamon

1 teaspoon grated nutmeg

½ teaspoon salt

1¼ cups buttermilk

½ cup maple syrup

6 tablespoons unsalted butter, melted

2 large eggs, lightly beaten

2 teaspoons vanilla extract

½ cup dried cranberries, chopped

¼ cup unsalted, toasted sunflower seeds

Preheat the oven to 375°F. Generously grease a 12-cup muffin tin.

In a large bowl, whisk together flour, wheat bran, baking powder, baking soda, cinnamon, nutmeg, and salt.

In a separate bowl, whisk together buttermilk, maple syrup, butter, eggs, and vanilla. Turn the buttermilk mixture into the flour and, using a rubber spatula, gently stir to just combine. Fold in the cranberries.

Spoon the batter evenly into muffin cups and sprinkle with sunflower seeds. Bake until a toothpick inserted into the center of the muffins comes up clean, about 16 to 20 minutes. Let the muffins cool for a few minutes before removing from muffin tin and cooling on wire racks (or enjoying as soon as possible).

SWEET TIP: No buttermilk? Feel free to substitute an equal amount of plain (unsweetened) yogurt. Or whisk together in a small bowl 1 tablespoon of vinegar to 1¼ cups of milk and allow it to stand for about 2 minutes. Proceed with the recipe.

SWEET TIP: Use a very dark maple syrup for the most flavor in these muffins.

Maple Scones, with
Strawberry–Cranberry
Ginger Orange Jam.

MAPLE SCONES

Makes 8 scones

Maple shines through these crumbly, robust scones. Serve them warm with plenty of sweet butter and a strong cup of coffee or black tea.

1 cup whole-wheat flour

1 cup white flour, or more as needed

2 tablespoons maple sugar

2 teaspoons baking powder

¼ teaspoon salt

½ cup (1 stick) unsalted butter, chilled

½ cup toasted, chopped hazelnuts or walnuts (page 33)

⅓ cup maple syrup

1 large egg

2 tablespoons cream, or more if needed

Butter or vegetable oil for greasing the pan

MAPLE GLAZE (optional)

3 tablespoons maple syrup

1 tablespoon unsalted butter

Pinch of salt

Preheat the oven to 400°F. In a large bowl, stir together whole-wheat and white flours, sugar, baking powder, and salt. Using a pastry blender, two knives, or your fingertips, cut the butter into small pieces and add to the flour mixture until it resembles fine crumbs.

Stir in nuts, maple syrup, egg, and just enough of the cream so that the dough forms a ball. Turn the dough onto a lightly floured surface and gently roll in a little flour to coat. Knead the dough lightly. Transfer to a lightly greased baking sheet and pat into an 8-inch disk and cut into eight wedges, but do not separate.

Bake until golden brown, about 20 minutes. Remove from the baking sheet, carefully separate, and set on a rack. Drizzle with glaze and serve warm.

To make the maple glaze: In a small saucepan, stir together the maple syrup and butter over low heat, with a pinch of salt to taste. Bring to a boil and reduce the liquid by half. Spoon over warm scones before serving.

SWEET TIP: Use a dark maple syrup in this recipe.

HONEY BUNS

Makes 24 buns

The tantalizing aroma as these buns bake will drift through the house, drawing everyone out of bed and into the kitchen. They are irresistible.

DOUGH
- 1 cup milk
- 3 tablespoons butter
- 2 tablespoons honey
- 1 teaspoon vanilla extract
- 1 package (or scant tablespoon) active dry yeast
- 2 cups warm water (105°F to 115°F)
- 6 to 6¼ cups unbleached all-purpose flour
- 2 eggs
- 2 teaspoons salt

FILLING
- ¼ cup honey
- 1 teaspoon cinnamon
- ½ cup finely chopped pecans

GLAZE
- ½ cup honey
- ½ stick (4 tablespoons) butter

Dough: In a saucepan set over medium heat, scald the milk, bringing it just to a boil and then remove it from the heat. Add the butter, honey, and vanilla. Set aside to cool to room temperature.

In a large bowl, proof the yeast by dissolving it in the water for about 5 minutes, or until the surface becomes foamy. Add 2 cups of flour, beating it until the mixture reaches the consistency of mud. Cover the dough and set aside to rise for 30 minutes. While the dough is rising, make the glaze.

Add the milk mixture, eggs, and salt with 4 cups of flour to the dough that was set aside and combine until smooth. Turn onto a lightly floured board and knead 8 to 10 minutes, sprinkling with more flour to keep the dough from sticking. Place the dough in a lightly greased bowl, cover with a towel, and set aside to rise until double in size, about 30 to 35 minutes.

Filling: Mix together the filling ingredients.

Glaze: Put the glaze ingredients into a saucepan; set over low heat and simmer, stirring, until the glaze becomes thick, about 2 to 3 minutes.

To shape the rolls: Punch the dough down and turn it onto a lightly floured board. Cut the dough in half and roll each out into a long 9 x 13-inch rectangle and slather with the filling. Starting with the long side, roll the dough up into a log.

Pour the glaze into two 9-inch round or 9-inch square cake pans. Slice the log into rolls about 2 inches thick. Place the rolls on one of the pans, cut side down, on top of the honey mixture. Set aside to rise again for 15 to 20 minutes. Bake in a preheated 350°F oven for 40 to 50 minutes, or until golden brown and the tops sound hollow when tapped. Remove from the oven and serve warm.

SWEET TIP: To have freshly baked goods in the morning, make the dough and shape the rolls the night before. Cover and place in the refrigerator overnight, then pop them into the oven first thing in the morning.

Raisin Bread variation: Add ¼ cup raisins to the filling recipe. After the first rising, punch the dough down and turn it onto a lightly floured board. Cut it in half and roll each half out into a rectangle about 9 inches wide; sprinkle with half the filling. Repeat with the other rectangle. Beginning with the short side, roll each rectangle up and place in a well-greased 9-inch loaf pan. Allow the dough to rise 15 to 20 minutes. (Or cover with a large plastic bag and refrigerate overnight; allow to come to room temperature before baking.) Bake in a preheated 350°F oven for 50 minutes to 1 hour, or until golden brown and the tops sound hollow when tapped. Remove from the oven, turn the loaves out of the pans, and cool on wire racks.

HONEY MUSTARD GLAZED BREAKFAST SAUSAGES

Serves 4

8 **breakfast pork or turkey sausages**

2 **tablespoons honey**

2 **tablespoons whole-grain mustard**

Put the sausages into a skillet and set over medium heat. Sear the sausages until nicely browned on the outside and no longer pink within, about 5 to 10 minutes.

In a small bowl, whisk together the honey and mustard. Pour over the sausages and turn to coat. Continue cooking, turning occasionally, basting with the honey mustard until the sausages are sticky and coated, another 5 minutes.

SWEET TIP: Brush this honey mustard combo on pork chops, bratwurst, and chicken breasts to glaze them right before removing from the oven or grill.

Honey Mustard Glazed
Breakfast Sausages

MAPLE BACON

Serves 4

Serve this for brunch, at cocktails, or crumbled and scattered over a salad. It is delicious anytime.

---

8 **slices bacon**

2 **tablespoons maple sugar**

Preheat the oven to 400°F. Line a rimmed baking sheet with parchment paper and arrange the bacon in a single layer on top of the parchment. Bake until the fat is rendered and the bacon is beginning to brown, about 15 to 18 minutes. Carefully remove the baking sheet from the oven and sprinkle the bacon with the maple sugar. Return to the oven and continue baking until the bacon is browned and sticky, another 3 to 5 minutes. Transfer the bacon to a wire rack set over another baking sheet to catch any drips. Serve warm.

SWEET TIP: Try this with pancetta, the Italian version of bacon (cured but not smoked). It makes an elegant appetizer and is great for brunch.

Maple Bacon.

2

SPREADS AND TOPPINGS

These spreads are as delicious on morning toast as they are in a sandwich, on a scone, or whisked into a vinaigrette. Making your own spreads ensures that the ingredients will be 100 percent delicious: no fillers, no artificial colors, no preserving agents, no stabilizers. You can adjust the levels of seasonings, salt, and sweeteners to your taste. Most of these take just moments to prepare and many make terrific gifts. Stock up!

PECAN MAPLE BUTTER

Makes 1 cup

Here's a tasty spin on any nut butter. The pecans are toasted to become especially flavorful, while the maple adds a light, sweet note.

---

1 **cup toasted pecans (page 20)**
1 **tablespoon maple syrup, or more to taste**
Pinch of sea salt

Put the nuts into a food processor fitted with a steel blade and process, stopping to scrape down the sides, until you have a loose, thin paste, about 3 minutes.

Add the maple and salt, and process, stopping to scrape down the sides, until the spread is the consistency of peanut butter, about 2 minutes.

SWEET TIP: To make cranberry nut spread, process ¼ cup fresh cranberries into the pecans after they have become butter. Taste and adjust the seasonings.

MAPLE HAZELNUT CHOCOLATE SPREAD

Makes about ¾ cup

Not as creamy and smooth as commercial spreads but packed with plenty of real flavor. Spread it on a plain cookie or banana. Scoop and roll it in chopped chocolate to make hazelnut truffles. Or just eat it straight out of the jar.

½ cup hazelnuts, toasted

¼ cup maple sugar

2 to 3 ounces chopped good-quality, very dark chocolate (85 percent cacao), or to taste

Pinch of salt

Drizzle of vegetable oil as needed

Put the hazelnuts into a food processor fitted with a steel blade and process into a paste, stopping to scrape down the sides periodically. Process in maple sugar, chocolate, and salt to taste. If the paste seems too dry, add a little vegetable oil, a teaspoon at a time until you reach the desired consistency. Turn into a small crock. Store in the refrigerator.

SWEET TIP: To toast hazelnuts, spread the nuts out on a baking sheet and place in a preheated 350° oven until the skins crack and the nuts smell toasty, about 5 to 8 minutes, shaking the pan occasionally. Remove and turn into a clean dishcloth and roll to remove the skins.

SWEET TIP: You can also make this with almonds, pecans, and walnuts. Bake until the nuts smell toasty, about 3 to 8 minutes.

Sugar Maples—the Giving Tree

Sugar maples are critical to wildlife as well as to humans—white-tailed deer, moose, snowshoe hare, and flying squirrels are among the animals that feed on the maple seeds, buds, twigs, and leaves. Porcupines gnaw at the bark; songbirds, woodpeckers, and cavity nesters make homes in the sugar maples; and maple pollen is an important food for honeybees.

ROSEMARY HONEY BUTTER OR CREAM CHEESE SPREAD

Makes ½ cup

This spread is terrific on Jalapeño Honey Cornbread (page 117), a warm biscuit, or a delicate potato roll. Roll it into a log, then cut into coins to serve. It is easily frozen.

½ cup (1 stick) unsalted butter or cream cheese, softened

1 tablespoon chopped fresh rosemary

2 teaspoons honey, or to taste

Pinch of coarse salt

In a small bowl, cream the butter until smooth. Stir in rosemary; add the honey and salt, and stir until partially mixed. Turn into a bowl or spoon the butter onto a sheet of parchment and roll into a log, then twist at ends. Chill until firm. To serve, slice into coins.

SWEET TIP: Substitute freshly ground black pepper for the rosemary and maple syrup for the honey to make Maple Black Pepper Butter. Try it on baked sweet potatoes and squash; slather on a crusty whole-wheat roll.

Rosemary Honey Butter,
with Jalapeño Honey
Cornbread

STRAWBERRY–CRANBERRY GINGER ORANGE JAM

Makes 4 to 5 half-pint jars

Ginger adds zip to this sweet, tart tango. It's bright and pretty, a taste of summer on the snowiest morning. Maple adds a mellow woodsy note to round out the tart flavors. Flavorful Cara Cara oranges work especially well here.

1¾ pounds strawberries, cut into small pieces

½ pound cranberries

1 cup maple sugar

¼ cup minced crystalized ginger

¼ cup fresh orange juice

1 tablespoon orange zest

Place a small plate in the freezer for a set test. Turn all of the ingredients into a 10-inch sauté pan and macerate (soften), covered, for about 2 hours at room temperature.

Set the pan over medium heat and bring to a gentle boil. Lower the heat and simmer, uncovered, stirring and mashing the fruit with a potato masher or the back of a fork to release the juices for about 8 to 10 minutes. For a smooth jam, process with an immersion blender or pulse in a food processor fitted with a steel blade.

Remove the pan from the heat and place a dollop of the jam on the frozen plate. Return to the freezer for 2 minutes; it's ready if it holds its shape. If not, return to the stove to continue cooking.

Wash jars, lids, and bands in very hot soapy water and rinse well. Place the jars, lids, and bands upside down on a clean towel. Turn the jars over and add the jam, leaving ½ inch headroom. Wipe the rims with a clean wet cloth or paper towel; add the lids and finger tighten the bands. Cool, tighten the bands, and store in the refrigerator or freezer.

SWEET TIP: Frozen fruit works equally well here. Thaw before using.

BLACKBERRY GINGER MAPLE SAUCE

Makes about 3 cups

Make this in the late summer and early fall when fresh blackberries are abundant. Come winter, frozen blackberries work equally well. Spoon over crepes, ice cream, thick whole-milk Greek yogurt, or serve over slices of angel food cake topped with whipped cream.

1½ pounds blackberries, about 6 cups
¾ cup maple sugar
3 tablespoons lime juice
1 tablespoon lime zest
2 tablespoons minced crystalized ginger

Put all ingredients into a 10-inch sauté pan and gently fold all together. Cover and macerate at room temperature, out of direct sunlight, for at least 4 hours or overnight, until the maple sugar has drawn out juices from the blackberries.

Set the pan over medium heat and bring to a gentle boil. Lower the heat and simmer, uncovered, for about 15 minutes, stirring occasionally to dissolve the remaining sugar.

Skim off any foam that collects on the surface and mash the blackberries with a potato masher—or the back of a fork for a smoother sauce.

Wash jars, lids, and bands in very hot soapy water and rinse well. Place the jars, lids, and bands upside down on a clean towel. Turn the jars over and add the sauce, leaving ½ inch headroom. Wipe the rims with a clean wet cloth or paper towel; add the lids and finger tighten the bands. Cool, tighten the bands, and store in the refrigerator or freezer.

SWEET TIP: This works equally well with raspberries. It makes a terrific spritzer or vodka cocktail.

SIMPLE HONEY LIME AND BERRY SAUCE

Makes about 3 half-pint jars

This makes delicious use of summertime berries. Use any mix that's in season (tart cherries work beautifully, too). Serve over vanilla ice cream for a dessert worthy of any dinner party.

---

4 **cups berries or pitted cherries**
1 **tablespoon lime zest**
½ **cup honey**

Put the berries into a 10-inch sauté pan, mash them lightly with a fork, and add lime zest. Set the pan over medium heat and bring to a gentle boil, stirring well. Lower the heat and simmer, uncovered, for 10 minutes, stirring occasionally. Turn off the heat and let rest for about 5 minutes; stir in the honey.

Wash jars, lids, and bands in very hot soapy water; rinse well. Place the jars, lids, and bands upside down on a clean towel to drain. Turn the jars over and add the sauce, leaving ½ inch headroom. Wipe the rims with a clean wet cloth or paper towel; add lids and finger tighten the bands. Cool, tighten the bands, and store in refrigerator or freezer.

SWEET TIP: Use a mild honey in this sauce.

OVEN-ROASTED APPLE AND PEAR SAUCE

Makes 4 to 5 cups

Oven roasting the fruit saves time and the trouble of constantly stirring the pot. Plus, roasting seems to condense the fruit's complex flavors. The combination of apples and pears gives this sauce lush texture while maple vinegar adds a nice edge. There is no need to peel the fruit: their natural pectin adds body.

The sauce is just savory enough for potato pancakes, pork chops, and sausage, and sweet enough to top waffles and North Country Maple Granola (page 18). Serve it with aged cheddar cheese.

---

6 cups water

2 tablespoons lemon juice

1 pound ripe pears, cored

2 pounds tart apples, cored (e.g., Chestnut crab apples)

2 tablespoons maple sugar

1 tablespoon maple or cider vinegar

1 teaspoon ground ginger

½ teaspoon salt

Preheat the oven to 400°F. Combine water and lemon juice in a large mixing bowl. Coarsely chop the fruit, and hold in the acidified water to prevent browning. You should have about 9 to 10 cups of fruit. Drain the fruit.

Turn the fruit into a bowl with the maple sugar, vinegar, ginger, and salt; mix well with a wooden spoon.

Turn the fruit out onto a rimmed 13 x 18-inch baking sheet in a single layer (it should fit). Tightly cover the pan with foil and place it on the middle shelf in the oven.

Roast the fruit until very soft and tender when pressed with a fork, about 45 minutes.

Transfer the cooked fruit back into the bowl and mash with a fork or potato masher. For a smoother sauce, puree with an immersion blender or food processor fitted with a steel blade.

Wash jars, lids, and bands in very hot soapy water and rinse well. Place the jars, lids, and bands upside down on a clean towel. Wipe the rims and add the sauce, leaving ½ inch headroom. Wipe the rims with a clean wet cloth or paper towel; add the lids and finger tighten the bands. Cool, tighten the bands, and store in the refrigerator or freezer.

SWEET TIP: The acidified water is simply 2 tablespoons lemon juice added to 6 cups of water. It helps prevent the sliced fruit from browning.

Lemon Thyme Chèvre

LEMON THYME CHÈVRE

Makes ½ cup

Stuff dates or apricots with this lovely spread, or serve in a pretty crock with whole-wheat crackers.

½ cup chèvre
1 tablespoon chopped lemon thyme
1 tablespoon honey, or to taste

In a small bowl, cream the chèvre with the lemon thyme and honey.

SWEET TIP: If lemon thyme is not available, use fresh thyme and ¼ teaspoon lemon zest.

Quick Ideas for Honey

Honey–Almond Spread: Process together 4 ounces blanched almonds that have been toasted until just lightly brown, pinch of sea salt, 4 tablespoons almond or vegetable oil, 2 tablespoons honey.

Honey–Lemon Mayonnaise (for shrimp or chicken): Whisk together ½ cup good-quality mayonnaise, 2 teaspoons Dijon mustard, 1 tablespoon fresh lemon juice, 1 tablespoon honey.

Honey Tonic: In a blender, process ¼ cup fresh lime juice, ¼ cup fresh lemon juice, 2 cups water, pinch of sea salt, 2 tablespoons honey. Great for hydrating!

Infused Honey: Add to a jar of honey a few lemon peels, or a cinnamon stick, slivers of fresh ginger, or a vanilla bean.

MAPLE CRANBERRY JAM

Makes about 2 half-pint jars

Swirl this with whipped cream and mascarpone for a simple yet elegant dessert. Spoon it over scones, oatmeal, and bread pudding. It will perk up plain yogurt and sit pretty on a cheesecake.

---

4 **cups fresh cranberries (or, if frozen, thawed)**

½ **cup maple sugar**

½ **cup dark maple syrup**

1 **tablespoon fresh lime juice, and the lime halves**

1 **teaspoon ground cardamom**

1 **vanilla bean pod (seeds scraped out)**

Place a small plate in freezer for a set test. Puree the cranberries in a food processor fitted with a steel blade. Pour the puree into a 10-inch sauté pan along with maple sugar, maple syrup, lime zest and lime halves, ground cardamom, and vanilla bean seeds and pod, stirring well to combine.

Set the pan over medium heat and bring to a gentle boil. Lower the heat and simmer, uncovered, stirring occasionally to prevent sticking, about 15 minutes. Add water if the mix seems dry.

Remove from the heat and do a set test by placing a dollop of jam on the frozen plate. Return to the freezer for 2 minutes. If it holds its shape, remove the pan from the heat. Discard the vanilla bean pod and lime.

Wash jars, lids, and bands in very hot soapy water; rinse well. Place the jars, lids, and bands upside down on a clean towel to drain. Turn the jars over and add the jam, leaving ½ inch headroom. Wipe the rims with a clean wet cloth or paper towel; add lids and finger tighten the bands. Allow to cool completely before storing in refrigerator or freezer.

SWEET TIP: Dark maple gives this jam a robust maple flavor; for less maple and more fruit, use a lighter syrup.

TART CHERRY HONEY SAUCE

Makes about 2 to 3 half-pint jars

Such an easy sauce! Whisk a little into mayonnaise to dress cold chicken. Drizzle it over Breakfast Bread Pudding (page 19).

---

4 **cups pitted**
tart cherries,
about 2 pounds
unpitted, chopped
1 **tablespoon lime zest**
½ **cup honey**

Put the cherries and lime zest into a 10-inch saucepan and set over medium heat. Bring the mixture to a gentle boil; lower the heat and simmer, uncovered, stirring occasionally, for 10 minutes. Turn off the heat and let rest for 5 minutes; then stir in the honey.

Wash jars, lids, and bands in very hot soapy water; rinse well. Place the jars, lids, and bands upside down on a clean towel to drain. Turn the jars over and add the sauce. Leave ½ inch headroom to allow for expansion. Wipe the rims with a clean wet cloth or paper towel; add the lids and finger tighten the bands. Cool completely, tighten the bands, store in the refrigerator or freezer.

SWEET TIP: Cut cherries in the pan using a scissors: it's quicker and less messy.

Busy Bees!

Honeybees are becoming endangered due to a number of factors: colony collapse disorder, mites, deforestation, industrial agriculture. The loss of diversity in corn and soy fields and the industrial chemicals used to farm monocrops have had a devastating effect on bee health. Bees are critical not just to our food but as key players in our food system as prodigious pollinators of food crops, orchards, and backyard garden flowers. Greg Reynolds of Riverbend Farm, Delano, Minnesota, had to hand-pollinate eggplant one year because of a loss of bees on his farm. "The bees are much better at pollinating than we are," he said.

3

SNACKS AND NOSHES

Maple syrup and honey make a terrific glaze for nuts, popcorn, and dried beans, giving crunchies even more crunch. When you add a little of these natural sweeteners to your favorite recipes, they help amplify the flavors—salty, hot, spicy, and tangy. Here are recipes for healthy, satisfying munchies to pack for the trail, a road trip, or to give friends. Others make easy appetizers to serve with drinks and elegant little plates. Keep them all on hand for last-minute guests.

CURRIED CHICKPEAS

Makes 1 cup (easily doubled)

Dare I say that these spicy, crunchy, easy-to-make snacks might be too easy to make? Roasted chickpeas have about half the calories of toasted almonds and they are rich with protein, too. Eat them out of hand or toss them into a salad or on a soup.

2 **cups cooked or canned chickpeas**
1 **tablespoon sunflower or vegetable oil**
1 **teaspoon salt, or more to taste**
2 **tablespoons honey**
1 **teaspoon curry powder**
1 **teaspoon ground fennel**
Pinch of cayenne pepper

Preheat the oven to 400°F. Line a baking sheet with parchment paper.

Turn the chickpeas into a colander and rinse well with cold water. Lay them on a clean kitchen towel to dry and, using your fingers, slip off and discard the skin.

Turn the chickpeas into a medium bowl and toss with oil and salt. Turn them out onto the baking sheet in a single layer. Roast, shaking the pan occasionally, until they are golden brown, about 20 minutes.

While the chickpeas are roasting, add the honey, curry powder, and fennel to the bowl that should have a little remaining oil and salt, and stir to make a paste. Turn the cooked chickpeas into this spiced honey paste. Using a spoon, toss the nuts to coat well.

Reduce the heat to 350°F. Spread the coated chickpeas in an even layer and roast, shaking the pan occasionally, until they are nicely glazed and browned, about 10 minutes more. Cool completely before storing in an airtight container.

SMOKED PAPRIKA CHICKPEAS

2 **tablespoons maple syrup**
1 **teaspoon smoked paprika**
1 **teaspoon ground coriander**
½ **teaspoon ground allspice**

After tossing the chickpeas with oil, substitute the following for the honey and spices and continue with the instructions.

SWEET TIP: Do take the time to remove the skins from the chickpeas. They will roast evenly and retain the spice coating . . . and they're much prettier this way, too.

Curried Chickpeas, with
Smoked Paprika Chickpeas
and Savory Sweet Cocktail Nuts

SAVORY SWEET COCKTAIL NUTS

Makes about 2½ cups (easily doubled)

These make terrific gifts, wonderful snacks, and they are great scattered on salads and wild rice pilaf. They are a bit sticky—and they are delicious with a cold beer. Just be warned: once you start eating them, it's hard to stop!

Try many different variations with a range of spices.

¾ **pound mixed nuts, about 2½ cups**

1 **tablespoon sunflower or vegetable oil**

1 **tablespoon maple syrup**

1 **teaspoon sea salt**

1 **teaspoon sweet smoked paprika**

½ **teaspoon cayenne pepper**

½ **teaspoon ground coriander, or more to taste**

Preheat the oven to 350°F. Line a rimmed baking sheet with parchment paper. Turn the nuts onto the baking sheet and toast for 10 minutes on the middle rack in the oven.

In a medium bowl, stir together the remaining ingredients to make a loose paste. Turn the nuts into the bowl and, using a spoon, toss the nuts to coat well.

Turn the nuts back onto the lined baking sheet to cool, keeping them in a small pile. As the nuts cool, stir them again a few times to make sure the coating is evenly distributed.

HONEY–PAPRIKA NUTS

1 tablespoon sunflower or vegetable oil

2 tablespoons honey

1 teaspoon sea salt

1 teaspoon sweet Hungarian paprika

½ teaspoon ground ginger

½ teaspoon ground cardamom

After roasting the nuts, toss with one of the following and continue with the instructions.

SWEET TIP: Once they have cooled, store these seasoned nuts in an airtight container.

SAVORY ROSEMARY NUTS

1 tablespoon sunflower or vegetable oil

1 tablespoon maple sugar

1 tablespoon maple syrup

1 tablespoon minced rosemary

1 teaspoon sea salt

½ teaspoon smoked paprika

¼ teaspoon cayenne pepper

BROWN BUTTER HONEY POPCORN

Makes about 16 cups

Browned butter adds a lovely, nutty note. Try floating this rich, salty–sweet popcorn on corn chowder or squash soup.

2　teaspoons canola oil
½　cup popcorn kernels
4　tablespoons (½ stick) unsalted butter
3　tablespoons honey
1　teaspoon coarse salt

Put the oil and popcorn into a tall pot. Cover and set over medium heat, and shake the pot until all the kernels have popped. Pour the popcorn into a large bowl (removing any unpopped kernels).

In a large, deep skillet set over medium heat, melt the butter, swirling the pan so that it cooks evenly. Watch as it foams and the color progresses from lemony yellow to golden tan to toasty brown. As soon as you smell that nutty aroma, remove the pan and turn the butter into a small heatproof bowl. Stir in the honey until it's melted, add the salt, and drizzle this over the popcorn, tossing to coat well. Serve right away. Once cooled, store any leftovers in an airtight container.

SWEET TIP: In a rush? Make this with packaged unsalted popcorn or corn nuts.

Brown Butter Honey Popcorn

Savory Maple Black Pepper Biscotti, with Green Tomato Chutney and Hot and Sweet Cherry Relish

SAVORY MAPLE BLACK PEPPER BISCOTTI

Makes about 24 to 32 biscotti

Perfect for nibbling with wine or dunking in chai tea. Top these with Onion Maple Jam (page 75) and thick slices of sharp cheddar cheese.

½ cup chopped blanched almonds

2 cups unbleached all-purpose flour

¼ cup cornmeal

1 teaspoon coarsely ground black pepper

⅛ teaspoon cayenne pepper

1½ teaspoons salt

1¼ teaspoons baking powder

½ teaspoon baking soda

2 teaspoons maple sugar

½ cup buttermilk

2 large eggs

Preheat the oven to 375°F. Put the almonds in a baking dish and roast, tossing occasionally, until fragrant, about 7 to 8 minutes. Let cool; chop fine.

In a medium bowl, combine the flour, cornmeal, black pepper, cayenne pepper, salt, baking powder, baking soda, maple sugar, and the almonds. Make a well in the center.

In a small bowl, whisk the buttermilk with the eggs. Pour this into the well. Stir with a fork to create a crumbly dough. Gather the dough with your hands.

Transfer the dough to a lightly floured work surface and knead until smooth but still slightly sticky. Divide the dough into four parts and cover with plastic wrap. Working with one piece of dough at a time, roll the dough into a log that is about 2 inches wide and 12 inches long. Repeat with the remaining dough. Put the logs on two baking sheets, spacing them about 2 inches apart. Bake until golden, about 15 to 20 minutes. As they bake, the tops may split down the center. Cool on the baking sheets.

Reduce the heat to 200°F. Transfer the logs to a cutting board. Using a serrated knife, slice the logs into slices that are ½ inch thick. Arrange the slices cut side up on the baking sheets and bake until hard to the touch, about 15 minutes. Turn the biscotti over and continue baking until they are dry and very crisp, about another 15 minutes. Set aside to cool. These will keep in an airtight container for several weeks.

SWEET TIP: You can make these into smaller coins by rolling the dough into a thin log before baking. Once baked, slice very thin. Reduce the second baking time to 10 minutes per side.

MILLET MAPLE GINGER CRACKERS

Makes about 30 to 40 crackers

The millet gives these subtly spiced crackers a double crunch. Serve with Lemon Thyme Chèvre (page 41) or your favorite soft cheese.

1½ **cups all-purpose flour**

¼ **cup cornmeal**

¼ **cup millet**

2 **teaspoons ground ginger**

1 **tablespoon maple sugar**

1 **teaspoon baking powder**

¾ **teaspoon coarse salt, plus a little extra for garnish**

½ **cup water**

⅓ **cup sunflower or vegetable oil**

Preheat the oven to 450°F. In a medium bowl, stir together the flour, cornmeal, millet, ginger, maple sugar, baking powder, and salt. Whisk in the water and oil to make a smooth dough.

Divide the dough into three pieces. Working with one piece at a time, roll the dough between two sheets of parchment paper to be as thin as possible. Remove the top piece of parchment and sprinkle a little salt over the surface. Using a pizza cutter or sharp knife, cut the dough into diamonds. Leaving the crackers intact on the bottom sheet of parchment paper, slide the parchment onto a baking sheet. Repeat with the remaining dough. Bake until the crackers are slightly browned and firm, about 10 to 12 minutes. Remove and allow to cool. Store in an airtight container. To refresh the crackers, pop them back into the oven for a few minutes.

SWEET TIP: You can find millet in the bulk bin of most natural food co-ops. If it's not available, substitute sesame seeds or flax seeds.

FENNEL MAPLE HERRING

Makes 2 pint-sized jars

Aromatic and mildly sweet, this is great on a holiday buffet or as an appetizer served on toasted dark rye crackers topped with hard-cooked eggs.

---

1 small fennel bulb, quartered, cored, and sliced thin
3 shallots, cut in wedges
1 cup maple or cider vinegar
½ cup vegetable oil
½ cup maple sugar
½ cup water
4 bay leaves
1 tablespoon whole black peppercorns
1 tablespoon yellow mustard seeds
1 tablespoon coriander seeds
1 tablespoon juniper berries
1 teaspoon salt
¾ pound (12 ounces) marinated pickled herring, drained
4 large dill sprigs

In a medium saucepan, whisk together the fennel, shallots, vinegar, oil, sugar, water, bay leaves, peppercorns, mustard seeds, coriander, juniper, and salt. Set over medium heat and bring to a boil, then immediately remove from stove. Cool at room temperature.

Wash jars, lids, and bands in very hot soapy water and rinse well. Place the jars, lids, and bands upside down on a clean towel.

Pour the brine into two pint-sized jars. Add the herring pieces and place the dill sprigs on top and cover. Marinate in the refrigerator for three days before enjoying. These will store for up to two weeks, covered and refrigerated.

SWEET TIP: Be sure the brine is cooled to at least room temperature before adding to the jars.

Curry Marinated Herring,
with Fennel Maple Herring

CURRY MARINATED HERRING

Makes 3 cups

Icelandic Skyr adds a bright, tart flavor to the marinade, but plain yogurt will work nicely, too. Serve this on toasted dark seeded rye bread or sturdy rye crackers topped with hard-cooked eggs.

- 2 tablespoons rice bran oil or canola oil
- 1 heaping tablespoon good curry powder
- 2 tablespoons honey
- ½ cup plain whole-milk yogurt or Skyr
- ¼ cup good-quality mayonnaise
- 2 tablespoons minced cornichon
- 1 tablespoon drained capers
- ½ teaspoon salt
- 5 to 10 grinds black peppercorns
- ¾ pound (12 ounces) marinated pickled herring, drained

Add the oil to a small skillet set over medium-high heat; whisk in the curry powder until it infuses with the oil, about 1 minute. Whisk in the honey and transfer to a small bowl. Allow to cool completely.

Wash jars, lids, and bands in very hot soapy water and rinse well. Place the jars, lids, and bands upside down on a clean towel.

In a medium bowl, whisk together the yogurt, mayonnaise, cornichon, capers, salt, and pepper. Stir in the curry mixture, then gently fold in the herring pieces. Store the herring and the sauce in small glass jars in the refrigerator for up to two weeks.

SWEET TIP: Use a very mild honey in this recipe.

Herring—the New Lox

The briny tang of its marinade and the firm-fleshed fish are especially delicious served on dark rye bread. Like salmon, herring is a deliciously healthful fish, chock-full of omega-3, vitamin D, and antioxidants.

This marinade takes pickled herring to another level. The kiss of honey or maple sugar balances the acid and brightens the salty flavor of the fish.

CITRUS MAPLE-CURED SALMON

Serves 2 to 4

This simple recipe is easily doubled. It's fabulous on a toasted bagel with cream cheese, folded into an omelet, or served with coarse dark rye bread. Use a center-cut piece of salmon for even curing.

1 **pound salmon, skin on**
⅓ **cup maple sugar**
¼ **cup coarse salt**
1 **teaspoon lightly crushed black peppercorns**
1 **teaspoon lightly crushed juniper berries**
1 **teaspoon lightly crushed coriander seeds**
1 **tablespoon lime zest**
1 **tablespoon lemon zest**

Rinse the salmon and pat dry; set aside. In a small bowl, stir together the remaining ingredients.

Sprinkle about one-fourth of the seasoned mix into a small flat dish or roasting pan that fits the salmon snugly. Lay the salmon skin side down on the seasoning mix and sprinkle the remaining mix over the top, making sure the entire surface of the salmon is covered.

Cover the dish with a lid or aluminum foil and place in the refrigerator. Marinate for at least 24 hours or up to 48 hours, depending on its thickness. The spice mix will become liquid as it draws the moisture from the salmon. Spoon some of the liquid over the fish as it cures.

Once the salmon is cured, remove and scrape the remaining spice mix from the fish with a knife. Pat dry with a clean paper towel. To serve, slice thin.

SWEET TIP: Once cured, the salmon will keep in the refrigerator, covered, for up to a week. Slices may be frozen for up to one month.

Citrus Maple-cured Salmon, with Tangy–Sweet Maple Mustard Sauce

4

CONDIMENTS

Upbeat and on trend, these recipes spring from age-old traditions of creating condiments with honey and maple syrup. Both are natural preservatives with more complex, interesting flavors than white sugar. Stock up and keep these on hand to brighten a simple grilled pork chop, glaze a chicken breast, or perk up a cheese plate. Presented in pretty jars, they make wonderful gifts.

ASIAN GINGER HONEY SAUCE

Makes about ¾ to 1 cup

Made for slathering on roast chicken or pork ribs, dunking egg rolls or fried chicken drummies, this sauce can be whipped up in minutes.

1 tablespoon grated fresh ginger

2 cloves garlic, minced

¼ cup honey

¼ cup soy sauce

2 tablespoons sesame oil

2 tablespoons rice wine vinegar

1 teaspoon red pepper flakes

¼ cup green onions, sliced into thin rounds

In a medium bowl, whisk together the ginger, garlic, honey, and soy sauce. Then whisk in the oil, vinegar, and pepper flakes. Stir in the green onions right before serving.

SWEET TIP: Use a darker honey for a richer flavor.

Asian Ginger Honey Sauce

FERMENTED HOT CHILI SAUCE

Makes about 2 cups

Don't let the lengthy instructions dissuade you: this is one very special sauce. You'll need to be patient as the chilies ferment. But the heat and funk they contribute to the sauce's flavor are worth the wait.

- 1 **pound mixed red chili peppers, such as cherry bomb, red (black) Hungarian, Fresno**
- 2 **cups boiling water**
- 1½ **tablespoons sea salt**
- 1 **cup cider vinegar**
- ½ **cup maple sugar**
- 2 **tablespoon minced garlic**

Clean the peppers. Chop them coarsely and, working in batches, turn them into a food processor fitted with a steel blade and chop fine. Turn the chopped peppers into a very clean, well-rinsed quart-size canning jar. Dissolve the salt in boiling water and cool to room temperature. Pour the salted water into the jar. Stir to mix well.

Cut a piece of wax paper larger than the surface of the pepper mix; press it down to ensure that the peppers stay submerged in the water (the peppers may develop mold if exposed to air). Place the lid on the jar and finger tighten the band. Set the jar out of direct sunlight for up to two weeks in your coolest room to allow the fermentation to take place. Occasionally, loosen the lid a bit to release the gases accumulating in the jar and finger tighten again. After two weeks, the brine will be slightly cloudy and should taste a bit acidic.

Remove the wax paper and transfer the peppers with the brine to a 10-inch sauté pan; add the vinegar, maple sugar, and garlic. Set the pan over medium heat, bring to a boil, reduce the heat, and simmer, stirring occasionally to reduce the liquid a little, about 15 to 20 minutes.

Place a fine-mesh sieve over a deep bowl and strain the liquid into the bowl; reserve this liquid. Working in batches, turn the contents of the sieve into a food processor fitted with a steel blade and puree, adding the reserved liquid.

Once again, strain the sauce, pressing out the liquid with a spoon, and discard the solids left in the sieve.

Wash jars, lids, and bands in very hot soapy water and rinse well. Place the jars, lids, and bands upside down on a clean towel.

Turn the jars over and add the sauce, leaving ½ inch headroom. Wipe the rims with a clean wet cloth or paper towel; add the lids and finger tighten the bands. Cool, tighten the bands, and store in the refrigerator for up to three months.

SWEET TIP: A few notes of caution: be careful when working with hot peppers—their oils can sear your skin. Wear gloves and do not touch your eyes.

Do not attempt to process the entire batch of sauce in your food processor at once (the food processor is too small to hold it all): work in batches. Be sure that you use very clean, well-rinsed jars (free of any traces of soap).

Fresh Cranberry Honey Mustard, with Cherry BBQ Sauce and Maple Cabbage Fry with Juniper and Coriander

FRESH CRANBERRY HONEY MUSTARD

Makes about 4 cups (easily cut in half)

Mustard is the simplest condiment to make and a great gift any time of year. This soft blend doubles as a dipping sauce for pretzels, veggies, and kebabs.

½ cup yellow mustard seeds

¾ cup cider vinegar

¼ cup water

2 tablespoons maple
   pickled ginger syrup
   (page 72)

½ pound fresh cranberries,
   about 2½ cups

½ cup water

3 tablespoons fresh
   lemon juice
   (Meyer, if possible)

2 tablespoons minced
   maple pickled ginger
   (page 72)

1 tablespoon ground
   mustard powder

1 tablespoon lemon zest
   (Meyer, if possible)

2 teaspoons ground fennel

2 teaspoons ground
   coriander

¾ cup honey

Put the mustard seeds, vinegar, water, and pickled ginger syrup in a glass or stainless-steel bowl. Stir well, cover, and leave at room temperature for at least one day and up to three days to soften the mustard seeds.

Put the cranberries into a food processor fitted with a steel blade and pulse until finely chopped. Turn them into a 10-inch sauté pan and add the water, lemon juice, pickled ginger zest, and spices. Set over medium heat and bring to a gentle boil. Lower the heat and simmer, uncovered, until most of the liquid has evaporated, stirring occasionally, about 12 to 15 minutes. Turn off the heat and stir in the honey.

Cool slightly and turn the cranberry mixture and the mustard with the liquid into the food processor. Process for 1 minute, scrape down the sides, and continue processing until the mixture is thick, about another 2 minutes. Turn the mustard into clean glass jars. Cover and allow it to mature at room temperature out of direct sunlight for about a week before storing in the refrigerator.

SWEET TIP: Use prepared sushi ginger in lieu of the maple pickled ginger.

Honeybees!

Bees all have a role in community. The queen will leave the hive only once to mate with several drones. Worker bees protect the queen, gather pollen, and build and guard the hive. A healthy hive is a collection of overlapping generations.

TANGY–SWEET MAPLE MUSTARD SAUCE

Makes about ½ cup (easily doubled)

Feel free to adjust the level of hot and sweet in this bold sauce. It's terrific with the Citrus Maple-cured Salmon (page 58).

⅓ cup coarse-grain
   mustard

2 tablespoons maple
   syrup

1 tablespoon sunflower or
   vegetable oil

1 tablespoon lemon juice

1 teaspoon crushed red
   pepper flakes

¼ to ½ teaspoon salt,
   to taste

About 10 grinds of black
   peppercorns

Stir all of the ingredients together in a small bowl. This will keep for many weeks, so make a larger batch if you like. Store in a clean glass container with a tight lid in the refrigerator.

Quick Ideas for Maple Syrup

Spicy Syrup: Simmer ½ cup maple syrup with 5 ancho chilies; remove from the heat to steep an hour. Strain and store in a glass jar with a lid in the refrigerator. Drizzle over grilled and roasted meat or roasted vegetables, or whisk into a balsamic vinaigrette.

Maple Butter: Whip together ¾ cup softened unsalted butter with ½ cup maple syrup, a pinch of cinnamon, a pinch of salt. Store in a covered bowl or wrapped in parchment or plastic in the refrigerator for up to a month.

Maple Chèvre: Whip 2 tablespoons maple syrup into 1 cup softened chèvre. Serve on crackers or spread on pizza crust and top with chopped rosemary.

Maple Rum Whipped Cream: Whip 1 cup heavy cream until stiff peaks form, then whip in ¼ cup maple syrup and 2 tablespoons rum. This will keep overnight, covered, in the refrigerator.

CHERRY BBQ SAUCE

Makes about 3 half-pint jars

This is a sauce for turkey meatballs, sweet potato fries, and pulled pork sliders. Smoked paprika adds a lovely smoky flavor and a little heat.

---

4 cups pitted tart cherries, fresh or frozen

1 cup coarsely chopped onion

¾ cup maple sugar

¼ cup maple or cider vinegar

2 teaspoons ground coriander

2 teaspoons hot English mustard powder

1½ teaspoons mild smoked paprika

1½ teaspoons ground ginger

1 teaspoon salt

In a food processor fitted with a steel blade, puree the cherries and onion together. Pour the pulp into a 10-inch sauté pan along with the sugar, vinegar, coriander, mustard powder, paprika, ginger, and salt. Stir well to combine, and measure the depth using the dipstick method (see Sweet Tip). Place over medium heat and bring to a gentle boil, then lower heat a little and simmer, uncovered, skimming any foam that gathers on the surface and stirring until the volume has reduced by one-third, about 20 minutes.

Wash jars, lids, and bands in very hot soapy water and rinse well. Place the jars, lids, and bands upside down on a clean towel. Turn the jars over and add the sauce, leaving ½ inch headroom. Wipe the rims with a clean wet cloth or paper towel; add the lids and finger tighten the bands. Cool, tighten the bands, and store in the refrigerator or freezer.

SWEET TIP: The dipstick method inserts the handle of a wooden spoon or skewer into the liquid to be reduced: hold it straight and make sure it touches the bottom of the pan. Remove, and mark the "wet line" with a pencil. As the liquid cooks and reduces, insert the skewer or handle into the liquid again and note the new wet line. This will indicate how much the liquid has been reduced.

HONEY PICKLED GARLIC WITH LEMONGRASS AND GINGER

Makes about 2 half-pint jars

In late summer and early fall, our gardens and farmers markets are loaded with fresh, tender garlic. That's a good time to make this delicious, slightly sweet pickle. This will last for months in the refrigerator; you'll be grateful to have it on hand when the ground freezes and snow begins to fall.

½ **pound very fresh, peeled garlic cloves**

1 **2-inch knob of ginger, peeled and sliced into ⅛-inch coins**

4 **3-inch lemongrass stalks, split in half**

1 **teaspoon pink peppercorns**

¾ **cup cider vinegar**

¼ **cup honey**

Wash jars, lids, and bands in very hot soapy water and rinse well. Place the jars, lids, and bands upside down on a clean towel to drain. Turn the jars over and divide the garlic cloves, ginger coins, lemongrass stalks, and peppercorns between them.

In a small saucepan set over medium heat, bring the vinegar and honey to a gentle boil and stir to help dissolve the honey. Remove from heat as soon as you start to see small bubbles; pour the brine over the garlic.

Cover each jar with a square of wax paper slightly larger than jar opening. Fold down the corners with a clean spoon and push so some of the brine comes up over the wax paper.

Wipe the rims with a clean wet cloth or paper towel; add the lids and finger tighten the bands.

Cool completely, tighten the bands, and store in the refrigerator. Wait a few weeks for the flavors to marry and mellow before you enjoy.

SWEET TIP: If lemongrass is unavailable, substitute with a thin peel of lemon zest in each jar.

HONEY PICKLED CUCUMBERS

Makes about 6 half-pint jars

Honey adds a bold sweetness to this pickle. Use the familiar dill heads or substitute parsley seed heads. Use any thin-skinned, seedless cucumber in this recipe—English, Lebanese, or Persian cucumbers all work well.

About 2 pounds thin-skinned, seedless cucumbers
¼ cup coarse salt

BRINE
1 cup cider vinegar
1 cup water
1 tablespoon dried juniper berries
1 tablespoon whole coriander seeds
¼ cup honey
6 dill heads or 12 small parsley seed heads

Slice the cucumbers into thin rounds and layer them with the salt in a sieve or colander set in the sink or over a bowl for at least two hours, or covered in the refrigerator overnight. Rinse the cucumber slices well under cold running water to remove all the salt.

In a small saucepan, combine the vinegar, water, juniper, coriander, and honey and set over medium-low heat, stirring to dissolve in the honey. Bring to a simmer. Remove from heat. Set aside.

Wash jars, lids, and bands in very hot soapy water and rinse well. Place the jars, lids, and bands upside down on a clean towel to drain. Turn the jars over and add 1 dill head or 2 parsley seed heads to each jar before adding the cucumber slices.

Pour the brine and divide the spices into the jars. Cover each jar with a square of wax paper slightly larger than jar opening. Fold down the corners with a clean spoon and push down so some of the brine comes up over the wax paper.

Wipe the rims with a clean wet cloth or paper towel; add lids and finger tighten the bands. Cool completely, tighten the bands, store in the refrigerator for several weeks or freeze.

SWEET TIP: If parsley in your garden has flowered and gone to seed, clip and save those seed heads for pickles such as these.

MAPLE PICKLED GINGER (AND SYRUP)

Makes about 4 quarter-pint jars plus about 6 ounces syrup

Here's our northern version of the pickled ginger we associate with sushi. This recipe yields a bonus—fabulous ginger syrup! Try whisking the syrup into vinaigrette or shaking it into a bourbon cocktail. This will last several months in the refrigerator.

---

6 ounces ginger,
    peeled and sliced into
    thin coins
1 teaspoon sea salt
1 cup rice wine vinegar
1 cup water
½ cup maple syrup

Place the ginger and sea salt in a medium bowl and, using your fingers, mix the salt into the ginger. Let sit for about 45 to 60 minutes to draw out the juices. Then squeeze the liquid from the ginger and set aside. Discard the juice.

In a medium saucepan, stir together the vinegar, water, and maple syrup. Set over medium heat and bring to a gentle boil. Add the ginger, bring to a boil, then lower the heat and simmer, uncovered, for 5 minutes, stirring occasionally.

Wash jars, lids, and bands in hot soapy water and rinse well. Place the jars, lids, and bands upside down on a clean towel to drain. Turn the jars over and divide the ginger among the jars, adding syrup to ½ inch from the top.

Cover each jar with a square of wax paper slightly larger than the jar opening and fold down the corners with a clean spoon, pushing some of the syrup up over the wax paper. Wipe the rims with a clean wet cloth or paper towel; add the lids and finger tighten the bands. Cool completely before storing the jars in the refrigerator.

Pour the bonus syrup into a jar and store, covered, in the refrigerator.

SWEET TIP: If you're lucky, you may find locally grown fresh ginger during the farmers market season. It's thin-skinned and mild and makes a delicate pickle.

Maple Pickled Ginger, with
Miso Ginger Vinaigrette and
Fermented Hot Chili Sauce

HOT AND SWEET CHERRY RELISH

Makes 2 to 3 half-pint jars

Try this on lamb burgers or serve with your favorite soft cheese.

---

4 cups pitted tart cherries

2 teaspoons Harissa sauce, or to taste

2 tablespoons rice bran oil or vegetable oil

1 cup finely diced red onion

1 tablespoon minced garlic

½ cup honey

1 teaspoon ground fennel

½ teaspoon salt

10 to 15 grinds of black peppercorns

Put the pitted cherries and Harissa sauce into a 10-inch sauté pan and bring to a gentle boil over medium heat. Lower the heat and simmer, uncovered, for about 15 minutes, mashing the cherries with a potato masher or fork to break them up; stir to prevent sticking.

Heat the oil in a 10-inch sauté pan and sauté the onions and garlic over low heat. Cook until the onions soften and turn translucent but do not begin to brown, about 5 to 8 minutes.

Add the onion and garlic mixture to the cherries along with the honey, fennel, salt, and black pepper, and simmer for an additional 10 minutes.

Wash jars, lids, and bands in very hot soapy water; rinse well. Place the jars, lids, and bands upside down on a clean towel to drain. Turn the jars over and add the relish, leaving ½ inch headroom. Wipe the rims with a clean wet cloth or paper towel; add the lids and finger tighten the bands. Cool completely, tighten the bands, and store in the refrigerator or freezer.

SWEET TIP: Sea salt is our choice in all of the recipes because it is the most natural ingredient. Many of the commercial table salts contain anticaking agents or iodine that may discolor the fruit and vegetable in a pickle.

ONION MAPLE JAM

Makes about 5 cups

Although onions are not often associated with maple, this pairing emphasizes maple's woodsy notes and the onion's natural sugars. Try this on a burger or in bruschetta—or as the filling for an omelet. It's especially good with the Savory Maple Black Pepper Biscotti (page 53).

- 3 **tablespoons olive oil**
- 3 **pounds onions, medium diced, about 10 to 11 cups**
- 3 **tablespoons minced garlic**
- 2 **teaspoons sea salt**
- ½ **cup maple sugar**
- 2 **tablespoons maple syrup**
- ¼ **cup cider vinegar**
- 1 **teaspoon ground cardamom**
- 1 **teaspoon ground coriander**
- ½ **teaspoon ground ginger**
- ½ **teaspoon ground allspice**
- 10 **to 15 grinds of black peppercorns**

Heat the oil in a 10-inch sauté pan and sauté the onions and garlic over low heat with the salt. Cook, uncovered, until the onions are soft and translucent, stirring occasionally, about 8 to 12 minutes. Watch that they don't begin to brown. Add a little water if needed and cover the pan and continue cooking an additional 15 minutes.

Add the remaining ingredients and simmer uncovered, stirring to prevent sticking, until most of the liquid has evaporated, about 20 to 30 minutes. Taste and adjust seasoning.

Working in batches, turn the onion jam into a food processor fitted with a steel blade and pulse a few times until you have the desired texture, turning each batch into a large bowl. When finished, stir to ensure that everything is combined.

Wash jars, lids, and bands in very hot soapy water; rinse well. Place the jars, lids, and bands upside down on a clean towel to drain. Turn the jars over and add the jam. Leave ½ inch headroom and wipe the rims with a clean wet cloth or paper towel; add the lids and finger tighten the bands. Cool completely, tighten the bands, and store in the refrigerator or freezer.

SWEET TIP: Use whatever onions you'd like, yellow, white, or red.

GREEN TOMATO CHUTNEY

Makes about 4 to 5 cups

Here's what to do with the last of the summer tomatoes before the frost arrives. Try this chutney on cheeses, with curries, or to jazz up a simple chicken breast.

Let the ingredients rest in the pan overnight: this draws out their juices and reduces the cooking time, so you have a fresher-tasting chutney.

1½ pounds unripe (green) tomatoes, medium diced (about 4 cups)

¾ pound tart apples, cored and medium diced (about 3 cups)

¾ pound onion, medium diced (about 2 cups)

1½ cups cider vinegar

1½ cups maple sugar

3 tablespoons minced red chili pepper

3 tablespoons minced garlic

1 tablespoon ground ginger

1 tablespoon ground coriander

2 teaspoons salt

Put all of the ingredients into a 10-inch sauté pan, stir well, and let stand at room temperature for at least 8 hours or overnight.

Set the pan over medium heat and bring to a boil, reduce the heat to a simmer, and cook uncovered, stirring, until the tomatoes and apples have softened and the mixture is thick, about 30 to 40 minutes. It's ready when you can drag a large spoon across the bottom of the pan and the mixture holds its shape. Remove from the heat.

Wash jars, lids, and bands in very hot soapy water; rinse well. Place the jars, lids, and bands upside down on a clean towel to drain. Turn the jars over and add the chutney. Leave ½ inch headroom to allow for expansion. Wipe the rims with a clean wet cloth or paper towel; add the lids and finger tighten the bands. Cool completely, tighten the bands, and store in the refrigerator or freezer.

SWEET TIP: Use a good tart apple such as a Haralson or Greening.

SWEET CHILI BALSAMIC APPLE ONION CHUTNEY

Makes about 5 half-pint jars

Pile on sausages and burgers. Stir into mayonnaise for sandwiches. Set out as a dip for fries and chips.

- 2 **pounds onions, peeled, cut in half lengthwise, sliced into very thin half-moons**
- 2 **tablespoons olive oil**
- 1 **teaspoon sea salt**
- ¾ **cups maple sugar**
- 1 **teaspoon sweet chili powder (e.g., Aji Amarillo)**
- 1 **teaspoon crushed red pepper flakes**
- ¾ **pound apples, cored, and finely diced, about 2 cups**
- ¾ **cup balsamic vinegar**
- ½ **cup rice vinegar**
- 1 **tablespoon fresh lime zest**
- 3 **tablespoons fresh lime juice**
- 2 **bay leaves**
- 1 **teaspoon black peppercorns, crushed**

In a 10-inch sauté pan, combine the onions, olive oil, and sea salt; set over low heat, and cook, uncovered, until the onions become soft and translucent. Stir occasionally to prevent sticking, about 15 minutes. Be careful they don't begin to brown.

Stir in the sugar, sweet chili powder, and crushed red pepper flakes, and continue cooking uncovered for another 15 minutes, stirring occasionally to prevent sticking.

Add the remaining ingredients and continue to simmer over low heat, uncovered, until the onions are soft and most of the liquid has evaporated, about 25 to 35 minutes.

Wash jars, lids, and bands in very hot soapy water and rinse well. Place the jars, lids, and bands upside down on a clean towel to drain. Turn the jars over, discard the bay leaves, and add the chutney to the jars. Leave ½ inch headroom. Wipe the rims with a clean wet cloth or paper towel; add the lids and finger tighten the bands. Cool completely, tighten the bands, and store in the refrigerator or freezer.

SWEET TIP: Aji Amarillo peppers are less sharp and less harsh than most chili peppers—and just a little fruity. You can find Aji Amarillo chili powder at specialty spice shops or online.

5

DRESSINGS, SALADS, AND VEGETABLES

The key to bright salads and robust vegetable dishes is balancing contrasting flavors. The sweetness of honey brightens tart lemon or vinegar in a dressing. Maple brings a woodsy note to apple cider vinaigrettes. Unlike refined sugar, honey and maple syrup are viscous and so will add body to dressings and glazes for roasted and sautéed vegetables. Many of these dishes, when served in combination, make a satisfying vegetarian or vegan meal.

LIME, POMEGRANATE, AND HONEY DRESSING

Makes about ¾ cup (easily doubled)

Toss this into a robust grain salad and serve over dark greens; drizzle on roasted carrots, parsnips, and beets. It makes a terrific dipping sauce for sweet potato fries and grilled chicken. Because the flavors of this sauce are so bold, a little goes a long way!

¼ cup olive oil

2 tablespoons pomegranate molasses (see Oven-roasted Chicken Thighs with Pomegranate Molasses, page 132)

2 tablespoons honey

2 tablespoons lime juice

1 tablespoon minced garlic

1 teaspoon crushed red pepper flakes

1 teaspoon coriander seeds, toasted and crushed

1 teaspoon cumin seeds, toasted and crushed

½ teaspoon salt, or more to taste

Put all of the ingredients into a lidded jar, attach the lid, and shake vigorously. Store in the refrigerator.

SWEET TIP: Toasting the spices first draws out their aromas and deepens their complex flavors. Simply put the spices into a cold pan, set on the stove over low heat, and heat slowly so they release their scents. Watch that they brown a little but do not burn, about 3 to 5 minutes.

Lime, Pomegranate,
and Honey Dressing

SIMPLE HONEY GARLIC VINAIGRETTE

Makes about ¾ cup

This tangy–sweet vinaigrette is especially good on tomato, mozzarella, and red onion salad.

¼ cup olive oil
¼ cup maple or cider vinegar
1 tablespoon honey
1 tablespoon Dijon mustard
2 teaspoons minced garlic
½ to 1 teaspoon sea salt
10 grinds of black peppercorns

Put all of the ingredients into a glass jar. Secure the lid and shake like mad. Store in the refrigerator.

SWEET TIP: Use either sweet or coarse mustard here; coarse mustard adds a little texture.

HONEY MUSTARD VINAIGRETTE

Makes about ¾ cup (easily doubled)

Here's another great take on a honey vinaigrette dressing. Made with buckwheat honey, it's great on a salad; with light clover honey, it's terrific on greens or to glaze roast or grilled chicken.

2 tablespoons cider vinegar
2 tablespoons coarse Dijon mustard
1 to 2 tablespoons honey, to taste
½ cup nut oil (walnut, hazelnut) or vegetable oil

Put all of the ingredients into a jar and shake until emulsified. Store in the refrigerator.

SWEET TIP: Try a good-quality walnut or hazelnut oil for a richer flavor in this vinaigrette.

TAMARIND MAPLE DRESSING

Makes about ¾ cup (easily doubled)

The citrusy notes of tamarind, an iconic flavor in India, are tempered by the soft sweetness of maple in this lively dressing, sparked with lime, hot pepper, and ginger. Delicious with a citrus fennel salad or kale and pomegranate salad—a little goes a long way.

¼ cup vegetable oil
2 tablespoons tamarind paste
2 tablespoons maple sugar
2 tablespoons lime juice
1 tablespoon minced red or green hot pepper
2 teaspoons fish sauce
1 teaspoon ground ginger
½ to 1 teaspoon sea salt

In a half-pint jar, combine all ingredients and tightly screw the lid in place. Shake well. Store in the refrigerator.

SWEET TIP: Find tamarind paste in the spice aisle of most supermarkets and co-ops or online. It adds an earthy sour note to dressings and sauces.

Fennel and Sumac Dressing

FENNEL AND SUMAC DRESSING

Makes about ¾ cup

The tart, citrusy notes of sumac meet the anise taste of fennel in a complex dressing for spinach, jicama, cucumber, and edamame. Perfect on chicken as it comes off the grill.

¼ cup olive oil

¼ cup maple or cider vinegar

2 tablespoons maple syrup

1 tablespoon ground sumac

1 teaspoon ground fennel

½ teaspoon cayenne pepper

½ to 1 teaspoon sea salt

Put all of the ingredients into a half-pint jar, secure the lid, and shake like mad. Store in the refrigerator.

SWEET TIP: Sumac has a lemony flavor and is a popular spice throughout the Middle East and Asia. Find whole sumac and ground sumac in the spice aisles of grocery stores and co-ops, or online.

MAPLE CUMIN VINAIGRETTE

Makes ¾ cup

The perfect dipping sauce for fried sweet potatoes or cornmeal-crusted chicken. Toss with canned garbanzo beans and serve on dark greens. Use sparingly—a little packs a wallop!

¼ cup vegetable oil

2 tablespoons maple or cider vinegar

2 tablespoons maple syrup

2 teaspoons minced garlic

1 teaspoon ground cumin

1 teaspoon crushed red pepper flakes

½ teaspoon cayenne pepper

½ to 1 teaspoon salt

10 grinds of black peppercorns

Put all of the ingredients into a half-pint jar, secure the lid, and shake like mad. Store in the refrigerator.

SWEET TIP: Maple vinegar (fermented maple sap) is milder than apple cider vinegar.

Maple Vinegar

Maple vinegar is a wonderful substitute for apple cider vinegar. Milder and less acidic than apple cider vinegar, maple vinegar is pricy and not readily available, so look for it online. Whenever we can get our hands on maple vinegar, we substitute it for apple cider vinegar. As cooks become more aware of the value of maple products and ask for them from their favorite stores, we hope more producers will include maple vinegar in their product line.

Maple Vinegar

MISO GINGER VINAIGRETTE

Makes about ¾ cup

The umami notes of miso blend beautifully with the subtle sweetness of maple in this creamy dressing. Toss with spinach and strawberries, or with kale with apples or pears. Drizzle over sliced steak.

½ cup sunflower or
    vegetable oil
2 tablespoons miso
2 tablespoons maple
    syrup
2 tablespoons rice wine
    vinegar
    Salt and freshly ground
    black pepper to taste

Combine the first four ingredients in a clean jar with a lid. Seal the jar and shake until the dressing is emulsified and creamy. Taste the dressing and season with salt and pepper. Store in the refrigerator.

SWEET TIP: Use a mild white or Shiro miso in this recipe. Made from fermented soybeans, it has a milder flavor and is lower in salt than the darker varieties.

MAPLE CABBAGE FRY WITH JUNIPER AND CORIANDER

Serves 4 to 6

A terrific alternative to sauerkraut. Pile this on grilled sausages or pork chops.

- 2 tablespoons olive or vegetable oil
- 1 large onion, sliced into thin half moons
- 1 teaspoon juniper berries, crushed
- 1 teaspoon coriander seeds, crushed
- 1 large tart apple, cored and sliced thin
- 2 tablespoons maple or rice vinegar
- 2 tablespoons maple syrup
- 1 teaspoon salt
- 10 to 15 grinds of black peppercorns
- 1 small green cabbage, about 2 pounds, coarsely shredded
- 5 large sage leaves, minced
- 1 tablespoon good-quality balsamic vinegar

Heat the oil in a large, deep, covered skillet over medium-low heat; add the onions, juniper, and coriander. Stir, cover, and cook slowly until the onion is soft and just beginning to color, about 8 to 10 minutes.

Stir in the apple, maple or rice vinegar, maple syrup, salt, and pepper and cook until the apple softens, about 3 to 5 minutes.

Add the cabbage. Stir and cover; increase the heat to medium. Cook until soft and beginning to brown, about 20 minutes. If the cabbage is too moist, remove the lid and continue cooking until no liquid is left in the pan. Remove from the heat. Toss in the sage and drizzle with the balsamic vinegar.

SWEET TIP: Substitute red, savoy, or Napa cabbage in this recipe.

Garlicky Kale

GARLICKY COLLARDS OR KALE

Serves 4 to 6

Cut into thin ribbons, collard greens cook immediately. Seasoned with maple vinegar and hot pepper, they are hot and sweet and great with scrambled eggs or alongside a grilled pork chop.

---

2 **tablespoons maple or cider vinegar**

1 **to 2 tablespoons honey, to taste**

2 **pounds collard greens or kale**

3 **tablespoons sunflower or vegetable oil**

6 **cloves garlic, smashed and peeled**
   Generous pinch of red pepper flakes
   Coarse salt

In a small bowl, whisk together the vinegar and honey.

Trim the stems from the collard leaves; then divide each leaf in half lengthwise and cut away the stem. Wash and pat dry the leaves. Stack the leaves and roll up tightly to form a cigar. Using a sharp knife, cut the leaves into ¼-inch thick slices.

In a large skillet, heat the oil and sauté the garlic over low heat until it's fragrant and golden; remove and set aside. Add the pepper flakes, then the greens and a generous sprinkling of salt. Using tongs, stir and toss the greens until they are coated with oil while cooking until wilted, about 1 minute. Remove and toss the garlic back in along with the honey vinegar and serve immediately.

SWEET TIP: Shredded green cabbage is also delicious cooked this way.

TANGY–SWEET GLAZED ROASTED ROOTS

Serves 4 to 6

This three-step process guarantees that the vegetables will emerge from the oven beautifully glazed. You can make these ahead and reheat in a skillet over medium heat.

½ cup honey

2 medium carrots, cut into ½-inch dice

2 medium parsnips, cut into ½-inch dice

1 medium turnip, cut into ½-inch dice

1 small rutabaga, cut into ½-inch dice

1 large shallot, cut into ½-inch dice

2 teaspoons apple cider vinegar

1 teaspoon chopped fresh rosemary

Salt and freshly ground black pepper to taste

Preheat the oven to 400°F. Cook the honey in a medium oven-proof skillet set over high heat until it is thick, dark, and bubbling, about 10 minutes. Stir in the carrots, parsnips, turnips, and shallot. Lower the heat and cook, stirring, until the vegetables become tender and are deeply glazed, about 8 to 10 minutes. Transfer the skillet to the oven and roast until the vegetables are caramelized, 15 to 20 minutes. Stir in the vinegar, rosemary, and a pinch of salt and pepper; taste and adjust the seasonings.

SWEET TIP: Because the honey loses any of its distinctive flavors when heated, it doesn't matter what variety of honey you use.

CAULIFLOWER WITH PERSIAN SPICES

Serves 4 to 6

A little maple amplifies the aroma of this warm Middle Eastern spice blend. Make this easy side dish into a dinner by serving over farro or brown rice and topped with Greek yogurt and chopped cashews.

---

1 head cauliflower, broken into florets

2 to 3 tablespoons olive oil
Pinch of coarse salt and freshly ground black pepper

3 tablespoons light honey

1 tablespoon za'atar spice, or more to taste
Lime wedges for serving

Preheat the oven to 400°F. Toss the cauliflower with enough olive oil to generously coat, along with the salt and pepper. Spread on a baking sheet. Roast until the cauliflower is nicely browned, about 30 to 40 minutes. Remove and turn into a bowl and toss with the remaining ingredients. Adjust the seasonings and serve with wedges of lime.

SWEET TIP: Za'atar is a traditional Mediterranean spice blend made with dried herbs (thyme and oregano), sesame seeds, sumac, and salt. You can find it in the spice aisle of the grocery store or online, or you can substitute an Italian or Mediterranean spice blend.

TOASTY BRUSSELS SPROUTS WITH HAZELNUTS

Serves 4 to 6

These make a terrific starter, side dish, and pizza topper. Try substituting broccoli or cauliflower for the brussels sprouts.

1½ **pounds brussels sprouts**
¼ **cup olive oil**
½ **teaspoon coarse salt**
  Several grinds of black peppercorns
2 **tablespoons maple syrup**
½ **cup toasted hazelnuts, coarsely chopped (page 33)**

Preheat the oven to 400°F. Remove any yellow or brown outer leaves from the brussels sprouts and cut in half. In a large bowl, combine the brussels sprouts, oil, salt, and pepper. Spread on a large baking sheet. Roast until the brussels sprouts begin to turn brown and crisp, about 15 minutes. Drizzle with maple syrup to coat the brussels sprouts. Continue roasting until very tender and dark brown, about 15 more minutes. Total roasting time will be about 30 minutes. Add the hazelnuts. Serve hot.

SWEET TIP: Use a dark maple syrup for a more robust flavor.

OLD-FASHIONED CORN PUDDING

Serves 4 to 6

Make this when the corn is fresh and sweet and use a good-quality cornmeal from a local miller. Serve as a side dish or a light main dish with a salad.

¼ cup unsalted butter, melted

2 cups corn kernels (about 2 to 3 ears)

½ cup light maple syrup

Generous pinch of salt

2 eggs

1 cup whole milk or cream

½ cup cornmeal

2 teaspoons baking powder

½ teaspoon freshly grated nutmeg

Generous pinch of salt

Preheat the oven to 350°F. Generously butter a 1- to 1½-quart baking dish with some of the butter. In a food processor fitted with a steel blade, pulse the kernels, maple syrup, and salt to break up the kernels. Then add the eggs, milk, and remaining melted butter and process until smooth. Pulse in the cornmeal, baking powder, nutmeg, and a generous pinch of salt until everything is thoroughly combined.

Turn the mixture into the prepared dish and bake until a knife inserted into the center of the pudding comes up clean, about 30 to 40 minutes. The pudding should be set but still jiggle a little. Serve hot.

SWEET TIP: In the middle of winter, use good-quality frozen corn, thawed and drained.

CURRIED CARROTS

Serves 4 to 6

Serve these alongside a rotisserie chicken (if you don't pick them right out of the pan first).

¼ cup fresh orange juice

2 tablespoons honey

1 tablespoon finely grated fresh ginger

1 teaspoon crushed red pepper flakes

1 teaspoon salt

10 to 15 grinds of black peppercorns

3 tablespoons olive oil

2 teaspoons curry powder

2 teaspoons ground cumin

2 pounds carrots, scrubbed, sliced diagonally ¼ inch thick

½ cup chopped cilantro

In a small bowl, whisk together the orange juice, honey, ginger, pepper flakes, salt, and pepper. Set aside.

Heat the oil in a large skillet over medium-high heat; add the curry powder and the cumin and cook for about 2 minutes; then add the carrot slices and toss to coat with the spice. Cook, stirring, for about 5 minutes. Add the honey sauce and simmer an additional 2 to 3 minutes until most of the liquid has evaporated and the carrots are coated and sticky. Remove from the heat and stir in the cilantro.

SWEET TIP: Substitute parsnips for the carrots, or use a mix of vegetables.

Curried Carrots

SWEET POTATO AND PEAR SOUFFLÉ

Serves 6 to 8

This is a terrifically versatile recipe that works equally well with butternut squash or pumpkin. Substitute apples or apricots for the pears and try other herbs, such as mint, marjoram, or parsley.

---

2 large sweet potatoes

¼ cup unsalted butter, plus more for buttering the soufflé dish

4 pears, peeled, cored, and cut into ¼-inch pieces

Generous pinch of grated nutmeg

Generous pinch of red pepper flakes

3 tablespoons maple syrup

4 shallots, finely chopped

2 teaspoons fresh thyme

Salt and freshly ground black pepper

2 tablespoons flour

1 cup whole milk

¾ cup grated Gruyère cheese

5 large eggs, separated

Peel and cut the sweet potatoes into 1-inch chunks and put into a large saucepan; add enough water to completely cover the potato chunks. Set over high heat, bring to a boil, reduce the heat, and simmer until very tender when pierced with the tip of a knife, about 15 to 20 minutes. Drain and set aside.

Melt 1 tablespoon of butter in a large skillet set over medium heat and sauté the pears until soft and golden, about 15 to 20 minutes. Stir in the maple syrup and cook, stirring until the pears are coated and very soft, about 3 to 5 minutes.

In a food processor fitted with a steel blade, puree the sweet potatoes and pears with the nutmeg and red pepper, then transfer to a bowl and set aside.

Preheat the oven to 375°F. Butter a 2-quart soufflé baking dish and set aside.

In a medium saucepan, melt the remaining butter over medium heat. Add the shallots and thyme, season with salt and pepper, and cook until the shallots are soft, about 5 minutes. Stir in the flour and cook, stirring constantly, until it no longer tastes "raw," about 3 minutes.

Gradually whisk in the milk and bring to a simmer, whisking constantly until thickened, about 2 minutes. Remove from the heat and stir in the cheese; season with salt and pepper. Whisk in the sweet potato and pear mixture, then one egg yolk at a time.

In a separate bowl, beat the egg whites until stiff peaks form. Whisk one-fourth of the whites into the cheese and sweet potato–pear mixture. Using a spatula, gently fold in the rest.

Place the soufflé baking dish on a baking sheet. Turn the mixture into the prepared dish, smoothing out the top. Bake until puffy and golden brown, about 35 to 40 minutes. Serve immediately.

SWEET TIP: You may also bake this in individual soufflé cups; reduce the cooking time by 10 minutes.

WINTER SALAD OF ROASTED SQUASH WITH MAPLE PICKLED SHALLOTS

Serves 8

Make this salad for a special dinner. It involves a number of steps but is well worth the time and effort. Plus, you'll be rewarded with extra marinated shallots–delicious tossed with cooked grains, served with cheeses, or on top of roasted chicken or pork.

SQUASH

- 3 **pounds butternut squash**
- 2 **tablespoons olive oil**
- 1 **tablespoon maple or cider vinegar**
- 1 **teaspoon coarse salt**
- 10 **to 15 grinds of black peppercorns**

SHALLOTS

- 1½ **cups maple vinegar**
- ¼ **cup maple sugar**
- 1 **vanilla bean, sliced in half lengthwise**
- 3 **star anise**
- 1 **tablespoon lemon zest**
- 1 **teaspoon salt**
- ¾ **pound shallots, peeled and cut into wedges**

SALAD

- 3 **green onions, thinly sliced**
- 4 **cups cleaned upland cress or arugula leaves**
- 1 **cup pomegranate seeds**
- ½ **cup toasted pumpkin seeds**

DRESSING

- 3 **tablespoons olive oil**
- 3 **tablespoons brine from the pickled shallots**
  Generous pinch of salt
  Generous pinch of freshly ground black pepper

Squash: Preheat the oven to 425°F. Peel the squash and cut it in half lengthwise. Remove the seeds and membranes. Cut the squash into ½-inch cubes. Toss the squash with the oil, vinegar, salt, and pepper. Scatter in a single layer on a 13 x 18-inch rimmed baking sheet and roast on the middle rack until the squash takes on a little color, turning occasionally, about 15 to 20 minutes. Remove and set aside.

Shallots: In a medium saucepan, stir together the maple vinegar, maple sugar, vanilla bean, star anise, lemon zest, and salt. Set over medium heat and bring to a gentle boil. Add the shallots and simmer, uncovered, until tender, about 12 to 15 minutes. Turn off the heat and set aside to cool. Strain out 1 cup of the shallots and 3 tablespoons brine; turn the remainder into a clean glass jar with the brine. Cover and store in the refrigerator for future use.

Dressing: Put all of the dressing ingredients into a glass jar with a lid and shake vigorously to combine.

To serve, toss the roasted squash, strained pickled shallots, and green onions with the dressing. Scatter the greens in a single layer and arrange the squash mixture on top. Sprinkle with the pomegranate seeds and toasted pumpkin seeds. Serve at room temperature.

SWEET TIP: You can make each of these components ahead individually and then assemble the salad right before serving.

Winter Salad of Roasted
Squash with Maple Pickled
Shallots

CRUNCHY CUCUMBER SALAD

Serves 4

Use any thin-skinned English, Lebanese, or Persian cucumber.

¾ **pound thin-skinned cucumber**

2 **teaspoons salt**

DRESSING

½ **cup maple or apple cider vinegar**

¼ **cup water**

2 **tablespoons maple syrup**

1 **teaspoon dill seed**

1 **teaspoon celery seed**

½ **teaspoon salt**

10 **to 15 grinds of black peppercorns**

Rinse the cucumbers and slice thinly, using a mandolin or sharp knife. Toss with the salt and turn into a colander to drain in the sink for about an hour. Rinse well under cold running water and press out as much water as possible.

In a medium bowl, whisk together the dressing ingredients. Toss the cucumbers in the dressing to coat. Marinate for at least a half hour before serving chilled or at room temperature.

SWEET TIP: English cucumbers are grown in greenhouses. You can find thin-skinned locally grown Lebanese and Persian cucumbers in natural food co-ops and farmers markets. These are crisper and drier than the large, seedy salad cucumbers.

CLASSIC WALDORF SALAD

Serves 8 to 10

No need to peel the apples: the skin adds a pretty color. This salad's components can be prepped several hours ahead and tossed together just before serving.

2 cups medium-diced celery

2 cups medium-diced apple, held in acidified water to prevent browning

2 cups red or green grapes, halved or quartered depending on size

1 cup toasted, coarsely chopped pecans (page 20)

DRESSING

1½ cups plain, whole-milk Greek yogurt or Skyr

2 tablespoons lemon juice

2 tablespoons honey

Dressing: In a small bowl, whisk together all of the ingredients and set aside.

Salad: In a medium bowl, toss together celery, apple, and grapes. Toss in just enough dressing to lightly coat. Add the pecans. Serve immediately.

SWEET TIP: Acidified water (a few tablespoons of lemon juice or vinegar in a quart of water) will prevent cut apples and pears from browning.

PICKLED GREEN CABBAGE WITH SWEET PEPPERS AND APPLE

Makes about 5 pint-sized jars

Pile this on grilled sausages, steak, and pork chops. It's the perfect dish for fall when local cabbages, apples, and peppers flood our farmers-market stalls. This recipe may look like it has a lot of steps, but each is simple and the boldly tasting result is worth the effort.

- 2 **cups water**
- 1 **tablespoon salt**
- ½ **pound tart apples, such as Granny Smith**
- 2 **pounds cored and trimmed green cabbage**
- ¾ **pound mixed sweet peppers (red, orange, or yellow), cored**
- ¼ **cup coarse salt**

SPICE MIX

- 1 **teaspoon crushed red pepper flakes**
- 1 **tablespoon yellow mustard seeds**
- 2 **teaspoons brown mustard seeds**
- 2 **tablespoons minced garlic**
- 1 **tablespoons coriander seeds, crushed**

BRINE

- ½ **cup maple syrup**
- 1 **cup water**
- 2 **cups cider vinegar**

In a medium bowl, stir together the water and 1 tablespoon salt. Core and cut the apples into thin slices, dropping the slices into the bowl as they are cut.

Cut the cabbage and peppers into thin strips and place in a separate large bowl. Drain the apple slices and add them to the vegetables. Massage the coarse salt into the vegetables and fruit to help release their juices. Cover the bowl and set out at room temperature away from direct sunlight for 24 hours.

Put the vegetables and fruit into a large colander and rinse well under running water. Drain in the sink.

Spice mix: In a large bowl, combine the spice mix with the well-drained vegetables and fruit, using your hands to be sure all the ingredients are coated.

Wash jars, lids, and bands in very hot soapy water; rinse well. Place the jars, lids, and bands upside down on a clean towel to drain. Turn the jars over and lightly pack the vegetables and fruit in the jars, filling them to about 1 inch from the top.

Brine: Combine the brine ingredients in a small saucepan and bring to a gentle boil. Pour the hot brine over the vegetables and fruit, leaving ½ inch headroom.

Cover each jar with a square of wax paper slightly larger than jar opening. Fold down the corners with a clean spoon and push so some of the brine comes up over the wax paper. Wipe the rims with a clean, wet cloth or paper towel; add the lids and finger tighten the bands. Cool completely; tighten the bands, and store in the refrigerator.

SWEET TIP: Find mustard seeds in the spice aisle or bulk bins of the co-op, grocery store, spice store, or online.

6

GLORIOUS GRAINS

Whole grains (farro, wild rice, quinoa, brown rice, and millet) are slightly nutty, chewy, and substantial, the perfect foil to bold flavors from around the world. Nutritionally, whole grains are a very sure bet, loaded with B vitamins and minerals. You can prepare them ahead and hold them in the refrigerator or freeze them for later use. With the addition of protein (cooked chicken, turkey, meat, tofu, or fish) these make a satisfying meal. Plus, they travel well to the weekend cabin, a potluck, or set out on the buffet.

WILD RICE AND CRANBERRY PILAF

Serves 6 to 8

Real hand-harvested wild rice from the clear, cold waters of northern Minnesota and Wisconsin is woodsy, nutty, and very fragrant. It cooks in no time (15 to 20 minutes), unlike cultivated rice grown with chemicals and harvested by machines. This pilaf comes together quickly; add a little leftover cooked chicken or pork for a hearty one-dish meal.

- 1 **cup hand-harvested wild rice**
- 4 **cups water (enough to cover the rice by about an inch)**
- 1 **tablespoon sunflower or vegetable oil**
- ¼ **cup chopped green onions, white and pale green parts**
  Grated zest of 1 orange
- 2 **tablespoons maple syrup**
- ¼ **cup dried cranberries**
- 2 **tablespoons chopped parsley**
  Salt and freshly ground black pepper to taste
- ¼ **cup toasted, chopped hazelnuts, optional**

In a medium saucepan, bring the rice and water to a boil. Reduce the heat; cover and simmer until the rice is tender, about 15 to 20 minutes. Uncover the pot, drain out excess water, and add the remaining ingredients, seasoning with salt and pepper to taste. Serve garnished with the hazelnuts if using.

SWEET TIP: To toast hazelnuts, spread on a baking sheet and roast in a 350°F oven until the skins are cracked and browned, about 5 to 8 minutes. Remove and turn onto a clean dish towel. Fold the towel over the nuts and roll so that the skins flake off.

Wild Rice and Cranberry Pilaf

FARRO WITH FENNEL, SPINACH, AND HOT PEPPER

Serves 4 to 6

Spicy, nutty, and citrusy, this pilaf makes a light meal or hearty side dish. Serve warm or at room temperature. It can be made ahead and travels well.

- 3 tablespoons extra virgin olive oil
- 1 onion, finely chopped
- 1 small fennel bulb, finely chopped
- 1 cup farro
- 4 cups stock or water
- 4 cloves garlic, chopped
- 2 teaspoons fennel seeds
- 2 cups fresh spinach, torn
- ¼ cup fresh orange juice
- 1 tablespoon orange zest
- 2 tablespoons honey
  Generous pinch of red pepper flakes to taste
  Salt and freshly ground black pepper to taste

Heat 2 tablespoons of oil in a saucepan and add the onion and fennel. Cook over medium heat until soft, about 5 minutes. Stir in the farro and add enough stock or water to cover by about 2 inches. Bring to a boil, then reduce to a simmer and cook until the farro is tender, about 30 minutes. If it gets too dry, add a little more water.

Heat the remaining oil in a skillet over medium heat; add the garlic and fennel seeds and cook for about 2 minutes. Add the spinach. Cover and cook until the spinach wilts, about 1 minute; then stir in the cooked farro, orange juice, orange zest, and honey, and season with red pepper flakes, salt, and freshly ground black pepper to taste.

SWEET TIP: Use a lighter honey in this recipe.

Farro with Fennel, Spinach, and Hot Pepper

Millet Salad with Avocado and Citrus

MILLET SALAD WITH AVOCADO AND CITRUS

Serves 4 to 6

Quick, easy, light, and refreshing, this salad makes great picnic food or an addition to a buffet.

---

1 cup millet
About 3 cups water
Generous pinch of salt
¼ cup extra virgin olive oil
¼ cup grapefruit juice
1 tablespoon honey
1 large avocado, cut into ½-inch dice
1 large orange, sectioned
1 small grapefruit, sectioned
¼ cup diced red onion
¼ cup chopped fresh mint
2 tablespoons chopped fresh parsley
Salt and freshly ground black pepper to taste

Rinse the millet under cold water and drain. Bring 3 cups of water to a boil and add a generous pinch of salt. Stir in the millet, reduce the heat to a simmer, and cook, uncovered, stirring occasionally, adding more water if needed, until the millet is tender, about 15 to 20 minutes. Drain and rinse the millet with cold water. Turn the millet into a bowl.

In a small bowl, whisk together the olive oil, grapefruit juice, and honey.

Turn the avocado, orange, and grapefruit segments, red onion, mint, and parsley into the bowl with the millet and toss with enough of the grapefruit dressing to generously coat. Taste; add more dressing if necessary and season with salt and pepper to taste.

SWEET TIP: This dressing also works well with any grain salad—cooked brown rice, farro, or cooked wheatberries.

Good Ole Baked Beans

GOOD OLE BAKED BEANS

Serves 6

You'll be the star of the barbecue with honest Yankee baked beans: this recipe is an authentic American classic. During the American Revolution, patriots shunned imported cane sugar and molasses and relied on home-grown maple syrup instead. You'll want to use the darkest maple syrup you can (graded dark or very dark).

2¼ **cups dried navy beans**
1 **teaspoon salt**
½ **pound slab or country bacon, coarsely chopped**
1 **large onion, coarsely chopped**
1 **large shallot, coarsely chopped**
¾ **cup dark or very dark maple syrup**
2 **tablespoons cider vinegar**
2 **tablespoons coarse Dijon mustard or mustard seeds**
1 **teaspoon freshly ground black pepper**
Boiling water
Salt and freshly ground pepper to taste

Put the beans in a large bowl and cover with cold water by 2 inches; soak for at least 6 hours or overnight; drain. Or, to quicksoak the beans, rinse them, then turn into a saucepan and cover with 2 inches of water. Set over high heat and boil for a few minutes; turn off the heat and soak the beans for about an hour; drain.

Preheat the oven to 300°F. Set a Dutch oven or flame-proof casserole over medium-high heat and cook the bacon until it browns and renders the fat, about 8 to 10 minutes. Remove the bacon and set aside to drain. Stir in the onion and shallot and cook until softened, about 2 to 3 minutes. Stir in the beans and remove the pot from the heat.

Stir the maple syrup, vinegar, mustard, and pepper into the bean pot and add enough boiling water to cover the beans. Cover the pot and bake until the beans are very tender but retain their shape, about 2 to 3 hours, adding more water if they look too dry.

Remove the pot from the oven, stir, and season to taste with salt and pepper. Increase the oven temperature to 400°F and return the uncovered pot to the oven. Continue cooking, stirring occasionally, until the sauce is thick and the top is brown, about 45 minutes to 1 hour. Scatter the bacon over the top of the beans before serving.

SWEET TIP: You can make this with canned navy beans. Skip the soaking and precooking steps. Simply add four 15-ounce cans of beans, drained, to the Dutch oven after cooking the bacon and onion.

MIDDLE EAST SPICED GARBANZO BEANS

Serves 4

Serve these nicely spiced garbanzo beans over farro for a hearty side dish or salad or with toasted pita bread for a simple appetizer.

---

2   **tablespoons extra virgin olive oil**
2   **cloves garlic, minced**
1   **medium onion, chopped**
1   **tablespoon za'atar seasoning**
1   **tablespoon honey**
    Juice of 1 Meyer lemon
1   **15-ounce can of garbanzo beans with liquid**
    Freshly ground black pepper to taste

Heat the oil in a medium skillet over medium heat. Add the garlic and onion and cook until tender, about 3 to 5 minutes. Stir in the seasoning, honey, lemon juice, and garbanzo beans with liquid and simmer until the liquid thickens, about 3 to 5 minutes. Season to taste with the pepper.

SWEET TIP: Find za'atar seasoning in the spice aisle of grocery stores, co-ops, spice stores, or online. This recipe also works well with mild curry powder.

JALAPEÑO HONEY CORNBREAD

Makes a 7 x 9-inch, 8 x 8-inch, or 9 x 9-inch pan

Robin Krause, food stylist, shared her recipe for her family's favorite cornbread dating back to her 4-H days in rural Kansas. It's rich and tender; just a little jalapeño gives this blue-ribbon winner a nice kick. We prefer a medium-grind cornmeal to give this texture and crunch, but for a softer texture go for the fine grind or use a mix. Enjoy warm from the oven, when butter is a must! It's great with Rosemary Honey Butter (page 34).

Butter for greasing
the pan
1 cup medium-grind
cornmeal
1 cup all-purpose flour
¼ cup cane sugar
1 tablespoon baking
powder
1 teaspoon salt
1 cup heavy cream
2 large eggs
¼ cup melted butter,
cooled
¼ cup honey
2 tablespoons minced
jalapeño pepper

Preheat the oven to 400°F. Generously grease a baking pan with butter and set aside. In a medium bowl, stir together the cornmeal, flour, sugar, baking powder, and salt. In a separate bowl, whisk together the cream, eggs, butter, and honey. Pour the cream mixture into the dry mixture, gently folding the ingredients together using a wooden spoon; stir in the jalapeño. The batter will be lumpy. Turn into the prepared pan and bake until it is golden brown, about 20 to 25 minutes. Remove and serve warm, cut into squares or rectangles.

SWEET TIP: We've made this in a toaster oven, cutting down on the preheating time.

SPICY SWEET ASIAN NOODLE SALAD

Serves 4 to 6

Asian rice noodles cook in a jiffy, so this salad comes together in no time flat. Adding cooked shrimp or chicken turns this into a main dish.

- 1 **box (8 ounces) of Asian noodles**
- 2 **tablespoons soy sauce**
- 2 **tablespoons rice vinegar**
- 1 **tablespoon fresh lime juice**
- 2 **tablespoons honey**
- 2 **tablespoons toasted sesame oil**
- 2 **teaspoons grated fresh ginger**
- 1 **garlic clove, minced**
- 1 **cup chopped cilantro**
- 1 **cup chopped unsalted cashews**
- 2 **cups shredded green cabbage**
- 1 **large carrot, shredded**
  Pinch of red pepper flakes to taste
  Salt and pepper to taste

Cook the noodles according to the package directions; drain and set aside. In a small bowl, whisk together soy sauce, vinegar, lime juice, honey, oil, ginger, and garlic. Add this to the bowl along with the remaining ingredients and toss to combine. Season to taste with red pepper flakes, salt, and pepper.

SWEET TIP: The easiest way to grate fresh ginger is with a microplane.

Spicy Sweet Asian Noodle Salad with Shrimp

QUINOA WITH WALNUTS AND DRIED CHERRIES

Serves 4 to 6

The earthy flavor of quinoa is sparked with lemon and honey. Serve this over dark greens for a light main dish salad or pair with roast vegetables, such as Cauliflower with Persian Spices (page 93) or Toasty Brussels Sprouts with Hazelnuts (page 94), for a satisfying vegetarian meal. This side dish also pairs well with Maple-lacquered Duck Breasts (page 136).

---

2 tablespoons extra virgin olive oil, plus a little extra for garnish
1 carrot, peeled and diced
1 onion, diced
Pinch of salt
1 cup quinoa
1 tablespoon freshly grated ginger
1 teaspoon ground cumin
2 cups water or stock
⅓ cup dried cherries
⅓ cup toasted, chopped walnuts (page 20)
2 green onions, trimmed and chopped (mostly white part)
3 tablespoons chopped fresh parsley
2 teaspoons grated lemon zest
2 tablespoons fresh lemon juice
2 tablespoons honey
Salt and freshly ground black pepper to taste

In a medium saucepan set over medium heat, heat the oil and sauté the carrot and onion with a pinch of salt, stirring, until softened. Add the quinoa and cook until fragrant, stirring, and beginning to pop, about 5 minutes. Add the ginger and cumin and cook, stirring for a minute. Add the water or stock and bring to a boil. Reduce the heat, cover, and simmer until the liquid is absorbed, about 12 minutes.

Remove the pan from the heat and uncover. Toss in the cherries, cover, and allow to sit for 10 minutes. Fluff the quinoa with a fork, then add in the walnuts, onions, parsley, lemon zest, lemon juice, honey, and salt and pepper to taste. Stir to combine, and drizzle in more olive oil to taste.

SWEET TIP: Vary the nuts and dried fruit; toasted almonds or pecans, and chopped dried apricots or cranberries also work well here.

PIZZA AND FLATBREAD

Makes 4 individual pizzas

We rely on freshly milled heritage grain flour from Sunrise Milling, Cambridge, Minnesota, and Baker's Field Flour and Milling, Minneapolis. The quality of the flour will make a big difference in the oven spring (the fast rising of the dough when it's first exposed to oven heat) as well as the texture of your pizza and flatbread. This recipe makes plenty of dough, enough for four small pizzas or flatbreads.

- 1 **package (or scant tablespoon) active dry yeast**
- 1 **cup warm water**
- 1 **teaspoon honey**
- 2 **teaspoons salt**
- ¼ **cup cornmeal**
- ¼ **cup whole-wheat flour**
- 1 **tablespoon extra virgin olive oil**
- 2 **to 2½ cups unbleached all-purpose flour**
  Extra virgin olive oil for oiling bowl, dough, and baking pan

In a large bowl, dissolve the yeast in the warm water with the honey. When it begins to foam on top, stir in the salt, cornmeal, whole-wheat flour, and oil. Gradually stir in the all-purpose flour to make a stiff dough. Turn the dough onto a floured board and knead for several minutes, adding only enough additional flour to keep the dough from sticking. When the dough is smooth and pliable, transfer it to a bowl that has been brushed with olive oil. Brush the top of the dough with additional olive oil (this keeps a skin from forming on top of the dough). Cover the bowl with plastic wrap; let it rise in a warm place until doubled in bulk, about 2 hours. Punch the dough down, turn back onto the board, and knead. Return to the bowl and allow to rise again for 40 minutes. Punch the dough down.

Divide the dough into 4 balls. Cover each ball with plastic wrap and allow to rise at room temperature for about 45 minutes.

To make pizza: Preheat the oven to 500°F. Put a pizza stone or baking sheet into the oven to preheat. Invert a large baking sheet and brush with extra olive oil. Place a ball of dough on the oiled baking sheet and, with your hands, spread and flatten the pizza dough into a 10- to 12-inch circle about ⅛ inch thick. Slide the flattened dough onto the pizza stone or baking sheet. Bake for 5 minutes, remove and add the toppings, return to the oven, and bake until the toppings are hot and bubbly and the crust is golden brown, about 10 to 15 minutes.

(continued on next page)

To make flatbread: Spread the dough onto a baking sheet and press or roll with a rolling pin to make it as thin as possible. Brush liberally with extra virgin olive oil, drizzle with a little honey, and sprinkle with chopped rosemary and a little coarse salt. Bake in a preheated 500°F oven until crispy and brown.

SWEET TIP: Don't feel compelled to make all the pizzas from this dough at once; dough can rest in the refrigerator for up to five days, ready to roll out as you are.

PIZZA TOPPINGS

3 **to 4 ounces fresh ricotta or chèvre**
1 **tablespoon honey**
1 **tablespoon chopped fresh rosemary**
2 **cups red grapes, sliced**

When roasted, grapes become sweeter. The rosemary adds a welcome piney note.

Bake the pizza dough until it just begins to color, about 5 minutes. Remove from the oven, spread with the chèvre or ricotta, and drizzle with honey. Scatter the rosemary and grapes over all. Return to the oven and continue baking until the crust is deep brown, the cheese is bubbly, and the grapes are soft and beginning to brown, about 10 to 15 more minutes.

Try topping the pizza with Toasty Brussels Sprouts with Hazelnuts (page 94).

Pizza, with Toasty Brussels
Sprouts with Hazelnuts

7

SWEET MAINS

These aromatic stews, glazed roasts, vibrant curries, and delicate fish dishes all owe their complex flavors and tenderness to the sweet kiss of maple and honey. Inspired by the ancient practice of creating boldly seasoned "sweet meats," these easy recipes are perfectly aligned with the way we cook today. Fragrant and satisfying, these dishes need little in the way of embellishment. Pair with rice, noodles, or whole grains and a green salad for a great meal.

SIMPLEST EVER VEGETABLE CURRY

Serves 4

Many wonderful prepared curry pastes are available that speed prep time on a busy weeknight. In this recipe, a few spoons of honey and lime juice give the curry a great kick. Serve this over rice or a mix of grains. Leftovers are delicious piled on pita.

1 tablespoon coconut oil

1 tablespoon red curry paste, or more to taste

1 onion, diced
Salt and freshly ground black pepper

1 cup vegetable stock

1 cup unsweetened coconut milk

1 small cauliflower, cut into florets

1 medium sweet potato, peeled and cut into 1-inch pieces

1 red bell pepper, seeded and cut into 1-inch pieces

2 cups cooked or canned chickpeas, rinsed and drained

2 tablespoons honey, or to taste

2 tablespoons fresh lime juice, or to taste

½ cup chopped unsalted roasted cashews, for garnish
Chopped fresh cilantro, for garnish

In a large, deep pot, heat the oil over medium heat and sauté the curry paste with the onion until the onion softens, about 2 to 3 minutes. Season with salt and pepper; stir in the stock, coconut milk, cauliflower, and sweet potato. Bring to a simmer, partially cover, and cook until the vegetables are just tender, about 8 to 10 minutes. Add the pepper and chickpeas, and season with the honey and lime juice to taste. Serve over rice or cooked grains garnished with cashews and cilantro.

SWEET TIP: Green or yellow curry pastes also work well in this recipe. Yellow curry is a tad sweeter than red; green curry is a tad hotter and the most distinctly Thai.

Simplest Ever Vegetable Curry

PAN-CHARRED HONEY-GLAZED SALMON SALAD

Serves 4

Use a strong, Creole-style mustard in the dressing for this boldly seasoned entrée salad.

---

2 tablespoons honey

1 tablespoon lemon juice

5 to 10 grinds of black peppercorns

½ teaspoon salt

1 pound salmon fillet, skin on

2 tablespoons high-heat vegetable oil, rice bran oil, or canola, divided

½ pound green beans, ends trimmed

3 ounces mixed greens

DRESSING

¼ cup olive oil

2 tablespoons lemon juice

1 tablespoon honey

1 tablespoon whole-grain mustard

1 teaspoon crushed red pepper flakes

½ teaspoon salt

In a small bowl, whisk together the honey, lemon juice, pepper, and salt and brush it on both sides of the salmon.

Add 1 tablespoon of the oil into a nonstick pan and set over medium-high heat. Place the salmon skin side down in the pan and cook until golden brown on one side, about 4 minutes. Turn the fish over with a spatula and cook until it feels firm, about another 3 minutes.

Wipe the pan with a paper towel. Add the remaining oil to the pan and return to the heat. Add the green beans and cook, tossing with tongs, until they are blistered and crunchy, about 2 to 3 minutes. Remove and set aside.

In a small bowl, whisk together all of the dressing ingredients.

To serve, divide the salad greens and green beans among four plates or arrange on a large serving platter. Break the salmon into small pieces and scatter over the top. Drizzle the dressing over all.

SWEET TIP: Use a mix of green and yellow wax beans to brighten the plate.

Pan-charred Honey-glazed
Salmon Salad

Maple Lime Scallops with
Cucumber Salad and Black Rice

MAPLE LIME SCALLOPS WITH CUCUMBER SALAD

Serves 4

Maple adds its woodsy sweetness to the sauce. Serve this over black, pink, or green rice for a visually stunning dish.

1 tablespoon lime zest

¼ cup lime juice

¼ cup soy sauce

⅓ cup maple sugar

2 tablespoons vegetable oil

1 tablespoon fish sauce

2 teaspoons crushed red pepper flakes

1 teaspoon salt

1 pound sea scallops

1 large English cucumber or 3 small Persian or other thin-skinned cucumbers, cut into ribbons with a vegetable peeler or into very thin slices

8 scallions, sliced

1 cup loosely packed cilantro leaves

In a small bowl, whisk together the lime zest and juice, soy sauce, maple sugar, oil, fish sauce, red pepper flakes, and salt. Pour this into a medium skillet over medium-high heat and simmer until the sauce has reduced slightly. Add the scallops and cook on both sides until they become translucent, about 1 to 2 minutes per side. Remove the scallops and set aside. Increase the heat and boil the sauce for a couple of minutes to reduce the liquid.

In a small bowl, toss together the cucumber, scallions, and cilantro. Place the scallops over cooked rice and arrange the salad near the scallops on the plate; drizzle the sauce over all.

Pairing Maple Syrup

Golden Color—Delicate Taste
- Glaze pork (including ham and bacon)
- Drizzle over shellfish
- In whiskey-based cocktails in place of muddled sugar cubes
- In Thai recipes as a substitute for palm sugar

Amber Color—Rich Taste
- Drizzle over hard and soft cheeses
- Top vanilla or chocolate ice cream
- Use in baked goods—breads, cakes, and so on

Dark Color—Robust Taste
- Great in coffee
- Terrific on aged cheeses (especially blue cheese)
- Well suited to baking
- Glaze red meats, bean dishes, root vegetables

OVEN-ROASTED CHICKEN THIGHS WITH POMEGRANATE MOLASSES

Serves 4

Fast and homey, this easy recipe roasts the chicken in a rich, flavorful sauce. Save any additional sauce for drizzling over leftovers and roasted vegetables.

---

1 tablespoon cumin seeds

1 tablespoon coriander seeds

⅓ cup honey

6 tablespoons pomegranate molasses

1 tablespoon finely grated ginger

2 tablespoons lime juice

2 teaspoons salt

1½ pounds skinless, boneless chicken thighs

In a small skillet set over medium heat, toast the cumin and coriander seeds until fragrant, about 1 minute, shaking the pan and watching that they don't burn. Crush the spices using a mortar and pestle or by turning into a plastic bag and crunching them with a rolling pin. Turn the spices into a small bowl and whisk in the honey, pomegranate molasses, ginger, lime juice, and salt.

Lay the chicken in a shallow dish so that the pieces fit snuggly in a single layer. Pour the marinade over the chicken; refrigerate for at least two hours or overnight.

Preheat the oven to 425°F and remove the chicken from the refrigerator and bring to room temperature. Transfer the chicken to a clean baking dish and drizzle with several tablespoons of the marinade; reserve the rest of the marinade for basting the chicken as it is roasting. Bake the chicken on the middle rack for 10 minutes, uncovered. Lower the heat to 400°F, cover the chicken, and continue baking, basting every 10 minutes with the reserved marinade until the juices run clear and an instant-read digital thermometer registers 165°F. Total baking time will be about 35 to 45 minutes.

Pour the marinade into a saucepan, set over medium-high heat, and simmer until the liquid is reduced by about one-third. Drizzle over the chicken right before serving.

SWEET TIP: Pomegranate molasses is pomegranate juice that has been reduced to a thick, intensely flavored syrup. You can find pomegranate molasses in specialty and ethnic food stores or online. Thick and rich, it's tangy with a musky flavor.

ROSEMARY KUMQUAT CHICKEN

Serves 4

The kumquats sweeten as they caramelize, adding pops of flavor to the straightforward roast. Serve with rice or potatoes.

---

1 **pound chicken thighs and legs, trimmed of excess fat, rinsed, and patted dry with paper towels**

¼ **cup olive oil**

2 **tablespoons honey**

2 **tablespoons chopped fresh rosemary**
Pinch of salt and freshly ground black pepper

1 **cup roughly chopped and seeded kumquats, about ½ pound**

Preheat the oven to 450°F. Place the chicken in a roasting pan or dish, drizzle with the oil and the honey, and season with rosemary, salt, and pepper. Scatter the kumquats over the chicken, allowing them to fall into the pan. Roast for 25 minutes; then reduce heat to 350°F and continue roasting, basting with any pan juices until the chicken is done, about 20 more minutes.

When cooked, the juices will run clear and the internal temperature of the thickest part of the chicken thigh will register 165°F on an instant-read digital thermometer. Total roasting time will be about 45 to 50 minutes.

SWEET TIP: Kumquats are sweet on the outside and slightly bitter within. Eat the entire fruit, skin and all. When roasted, they shrivel and brown slightly. You may substitute Meyer lemons here if kumquats are not available.

ROAST CHICKEN WITH LEMON AND TURMERIC

Serves 4 to 6

Lemon, ginger, and turmeric give this chicken a deep color and heady aroma. It's spicy, sweet, and loaded with flavor.

1 tablespoon lemon zest

2 teaspoons grated fresh ginger

2 cloves garlic

1 small jalapeño pepper, seeded, deveined, and chopped

1 teaspoon ground turmeric

2 teaspoons salt

2 teaspoons maple sugar

2 tablespoons sunflower or vegetable oil

1 whole chicken, 3½ to 4 pounds
   Sweet Chili Sauce (next page), optional

Put the lemon zest, ginger, garlic, jalapeño, turmeric, salt, sugar, and oil into a food processor fitted with a steel blade or a blender and process, scraping down the sides until a paste is formed.

Gently separate the chicken skin from the breast and spread the jalapeño mixture under the skin and over the breast meat; rub the remaining mixture over the entire chicken. It may be advisable to wear kitchen gloves while handling the jalepeño pepper and spreading the mixture. For best results, refrigerate the chicken, uncovered, for at least 2 hours or, better, overnight.

Preheat the oven to 500°F. Bring the chicken to room temperature. Place the chicken breast side up on a wire rack in a roasting pan. Put the chicken into the oven, reduce the temperature to 350°F. Roast the chicken, basting frequently, until the juices run clear and an instant-read digital thermometer inserted into the thigh registers 165°F, about 1 hour 15 minutes. Remove from the oven; allow the chicken to rest 5 to 10 minutes, uncovered, then carve and serve with the Sweet Chili Sauce, if desired.

SWEET CHILI SAUCE

Makes about 1/2 cup

Keep this sauce on hand to slather over pork and steak, or whisk into mayonnaise for a sandwich spread or into sour cream for a dip. Store it in a glass jar in the refrigerator for up to three months.

2 cloves garlic, minced

1 red jalapeño pepper, seeded and diced

1/2 cup maple sugar

1/4 cup white wine vinegar

1/4 cup water

2 tablespoons soy sauce

Combine all of the ingredients in a small saucepan, bring to a simmer, and cook until reduced by one-third and thick and syrupy, about 10 minutes.

MAPLE-LACQUERED DUCK BREASTS

Serves 4 to 6

Duck breast is one of the easiest, most satisfying cuts of meat. While recipes for red meat begin by heating a pan to smoking hot, the duck breast, with its hefty layer of flavor and lean red meat, calls for a much different approach. First, score the breast to encourage rendering; then place it skin side down in a cold skillet before you even turn on the burner. The slow heat gives the fat time to render and become crisp and golden, while the meat cooks to become juicy and tender. It takes just minutes.

¼ cup dark maple syrup
Generous pinch of crushed red pepper flakes
Zest from 1 orange
2 teaspoons chopped fresh thyme
2 duck breasts, about 12 ounces each
Salt and freshly ground black pepper

Preheat the oven to 400°F. In a small bowl, whisk together the syrup, red pepper flakes, zest, and thyme; set aside. Score the skin of the duck in a crisscross pattern, about half an inch apart, being careful not to cut through to the meat. Generously salt the duck.

Set the duck breast skin side down in a cold pan over medium heat. Cook to render the fat, being careful to brown but not burn the skin, about 5 to 10 minutes. Remove all but 2 tablespoons of the duck fat and store in a glass jar in the refrigerator for another use.

Once the duck skin is brown, flip the duck over and spoon on several tablespoons of the glaze, reserving the rest for glazing the duck as it is roasting. Grind some pepper over the duck. Put the pan into the oven; after 5 minutes, spoon on the remaining glaze and continue roasting the duck. The duck is done when an instant-read digital thermometer inserted into the center reads 160°F. Rest the duck for about 10 minutes before slicing diagonally with the grain.

SWEET TIP: According to the USDA, duck is cooked and safe to eat at 160°F, or medium, though many chefs prefer to serve it medium rare.

Maple-lacquered Duck Breasts, with Quinoa with Walnuts and Dried Cherries

DUCK CONFIT

Serves 4 (makes 2 duck legs and thighs)

This old, old method of slowly roasting duck in its fat yields a deliciously tender, meltingly rich meat. You may use this technique with chicken, pheasant, and quail, too. Once the meat has been cooked, it will keep for a couple of weeks if stored covered with its cooking fat. The maple at the end helps cut the richness and highlights the spicy black pepper and fresh herbs.

2 **duck legs with thighs attached**

2 **teaspoons coarse salt**

½ **teaspoon coarsely ground black pepper**

3 **cloves garlic, minced**

2 **tablespoons chopped fresh thyme**

2 **cups duck fat, or a mix of duck fat and vegetable oil**

1 **bay leaf**

2 **tablespoons maple syrup**

Using the sharp tip of a knife, prick the duck skin all over (trying not to poke through to the meat). Rub the duck with the salt, pepper, garlic, and thyme and place snugly in a glass dish. Cover and refrigerate for 24 to 48 hours.

Preheat the oven to 200°F. Remove the duck from the refrigerator, brush off the salt, and place snugly in a small clean baking dish. Warm the duck fat to become liquid and pour over the duck legs to completely submerge. If you don't have enough fat, add vegetable oil. Add the bay leaf. Cover the dish with foil and cook for about 4 hours until the meat is very tender and pulls easily away from the bone.

Cool to room temperature, then refrigerate for 8 hours or overnight. To prepare, remove the duck legs from the fat, scraping off any excess fat and the salty coating. Cook the legs and thighs in a cast-iron skillet, skin side down, until the meat is crispy, about 15 minutes. Flip over, and drizzle with maple syrup.

SWEET TIP: Duck fat is delicious. Once the confit has been enjoyed, strain the duck fat through a fine sieve or cheesecloth and store in a glass jar in the refrigerator. Use it to fry potatoes.

STOUT AND BUCKWHEAT HONEY-BRAISED BEEF SHORT RIBS

Serves 4 to 6

This recipe for braised beef ribs relies on buckwheat honey's rich, dark, funky flavor and a sturdy, smooth, and malty stout.

3½ to 4 pounds beef short ribs, trimmed
  Salt and freshly ground black pepper
2 tablespoons olive oil
1 small onion, finely chopped
5 cloves garlic, minced
2 tablespoons whole-grain Dijon mustard
¼ cup buckwheat honey
1 cup stout
2 sprigs rosemary

Preheat the oven to 350°F. Generously season the ribs with salt and pepper. Heat the oil in a heavy ovenproof skillet over medium heat and, working in batches, sear the ribs until very brown on all sides; set aide.

Remove all but 2 tablespoons of the fat. Lower the heat and add the onion and garlic and cook until they are lightly caramelized, about 5 minutes. Stir in mustard, honey, stout, and rosemary.

Return the meat to the pan and turn to coat with the sauce. Cover the pan tightly with a lid or foil. Put it in the oven and cook until the meat is so tender it falls from the bone, about 3½ to 4 hours. Remove the ribs. Skim the fat off the sauce. Reduce the sauce by simmering it over a high flame. Taste and adjust the seasoning, and serve the ribs with the sauce spooned over all.

SWEET TIP: Buckwheat honey gives this sauce a dark, slightly bitter edge, but you may use a lighter honey as well.

Bones to Pick

Ribs—pork, beef, and lamb—are not just for barbecue. They are delectably tender when cooked slowly in the oven with low heat. The recipe above and the recipe on page 142 call for braising the ribs by first searing them off in a heavy pan to create a crisp crust that helps to retain the juices, then roasting them slowly until the meat is so tender it falls from the bone.

Sticky Lamb Ribs, Hot and Sweet

STICKY LAMB RIBS, HOT AND SWEET

Serves 4

It's easy to forget about lamb ribs, but they are super easy to cook and finger-licking delicious. They're perfect for a casual supper, no forks necessary.

¼ cup olive oil

½ cup honey

3 garlic cloves, smashed

1 tablespoon chili powder

1 tablespoon smoked paprika

2 teaspoons ground cumin

2 teaspoons salt

½ cup rice wine vinegar
  Zest and juice of 1 orange

3 pounds (2 racks) lamb spare ribs

In a medium bowl, whisk together the oil, honey, garlic, chili powder, paprika, cumin, salt, vinegar, orange zest and juice.

Put the ribs into a large plastic bag and add the marinade. Seal the bag, pressing out the excess air. Place this on a plate and refrigerate at least eight hours or overnight.

Preheat the oven to 350°F. Put the ribs into a shallow baking dish and cover tightly with aluminum foil. Pour the marinade into a saucepan.

Bake the ribs for 1 hour. Meanwhile, set the marinade over medium-high heat, bring to a boil, and reduce the liquid by half.

Remove the ribs, spoon off excess fat, and pour the sauce over the ribs. Return to the oven, uncovered, and bake until the ribs are caramelized and sticky, about 15 to 20 minutes. Remove the ribs from the oven and let sit for about 5 minutes; then cut into individual ribs.

SWEET TIP: Lamb ribs, aka lamb spareribs or Denver ribs, are one of the most cost-conscious cuts of lamb. Substitute them for baby back pork ribs.

ASIAN PORK RIBS

Serves 4 to 6

A one-skillet, wonderful dinner. The sweet–spicy sauce infuses both veggies and meat with zest and flavor.

½ cup chicken broth

¼ cup dry sherry

¼ cup soy sauce

2 tablespoons honey

1 teaspoon hot chili paste (sambal)

2½ pounds boneless pork shoulder cut into thick strips (aka boneless country-style ribs)
    Salt and freshly ground black pepper

3 tablespoons vegetable oil

1 large onion, chopped

4 cloves garlic, chopped

2 tablespoons grated or minced fresh ginger
    Grated rind of 1 orange

2 tablespoons lime juice

In a small bowl, whisk together the chicken broth, sherry, soy, honey, and chili paste and set aside.

Season the ribs with salt and pepper. Heat the oil in a heavy deep skillet over medium-high heat. Working in batches, cook the ribs until browned, about 4 minutes per side. Transfer the ribs to a plate. Reduce the heat to medium; add the onion, garlic, and ginger and cook until soft and fragrant, about 3 minutes. Whisk in the chicken broth mixture, stirring to scrape up any browned bits. Add the orange zest and lime juice and return the ribs to the skillet.

Reduce the heat to medium-low, cover, and simmer the pork until very tender, about 30 to 40 minutes. Transfer the pork to a plate and tent to keep warm. Increase the heat and bring the liquid to a gentle boil; reduce the liquid by half, about 5 to 8 minutes. Taste and adjust the seasonings. Serve the pork drizzled with sauce.

SWEET TIP: This works equally well with baby back pork ribs and lamb ribs.

LAMB TAGINE WITH DRIED FRUIT AND HONEY

Serves 6 to 8

The term "sweet meat" is defined by this classic North African stew. It's very rich, needing little more than cooked farro or couscous to sop up the sauce.

½ **pound dried apricots, cut in half**

¼ **pound dried tart cherries**

¼ **cup olive oil**

4 **pounds boneless lamb shoulder, trimmed and cut into 1½-inch cubes**

2 **onions, chopped**

1 **tablespoon ground coriander**

2 **teaspoons cinnamon**

2 **to 3 cups lamb, vegetable, or chicken stock**

⅓ **cup honey**

Salt and freshly ground black pepper to taste

Put the dried fruit into a small bowl and cover with warm water to soak.

In a large, deep sauté pan, heat the oil over high heat and add as many of the lamb cubes as will fit without crowding and brown on all sides. Transfer to a deep, flame-proof pot or casserole. Repeat with the remaining lamb cubes.

Add the onion to the pan and cook until translucent, about 10 minutes. Then add the coriander and cinnamon and cook for another minute. Transfer the onion-spice mix to the lamb and add stock and enough water to cover the meat. Set the pot over high heat, bring to a boil, reduce the heat; simmer, covered, for about 45 minutes. Drain the fruit and add to the stew and continue cooking, uncovered, until the lamb is very tender, about 20 more minutes. Add the honey and season with salt and pepper to taste.

SWEET TIP: Make this a day or two ahead so that the flavors have time to marry. It is the perfect dinner-party dish.

8

SIMPLE FINISHES

Maple- and honey-sweetened treats are delicious, naturally. Their distinct flavors and textures enhance puddings and ice cream. They keep cakes, cookies, and bars moist and extend freshness after they are made. Drizzled over puddings and baked goods, these natural sweeteners make a fine glaze. As we all try to cut back on the amount of processed sugar we eat, honey and maple treats are a sweet reward. Eating well tastes good.

SCANDINAVIAN RICE PUDDING
WITH BLACKBERRY ORANGE SYRUP

Serves 4 to 6

This silky rice pudding is really a porridge. This recipe is a modern spin on a traditional holiday dish in Denmark and a perfect foil to the bright, tart blackberry syrup.

SYRUP

- 2 10-ounce packages frozen blackberries
- ½ cup water
- ⅓ cup maple sugar
- ⅓ cup orange juice
- 1 tablespoon orange zest
- 1 tablespoon vanilla extract

RICE

- ¾ cup arborio rice
- 2½ cups light coconut milk, divided
- 1 tablespoon vanilla extract
- 3 tablespoons maple syrup

Syrup: In a 10-inch sauté pan, stir together the blackberries, water, sugar, orange juice and zest, and vanilla extract. Allow the berries to thaw at room temperature about an hour. Set the pan over medium heat and bring to a boil, mashing the berries with a potato masher or the back of a fork to release the juices. Set a sieve over a bowl, turn the berries into the sieve, and strain for about 5 minutes, pressing the berries to extract the liquid. Discard the berries. You should have about 2 cups of liquid. Clean the sauté pan, return the juice to the pan, and set over medium heat and bring to a simmer. Using the dipstick method (page 69), reduce the liquid by one-half to one-third, about 5 minutes.

Rice: Put the rice into a sieve and rinse under cold running water until the water runs clear; then turn the rice into a medium saucepan with ½ cup of the coconut milk. Set over medium heat and bring to a boil, then stir in the remaining coconut milk and the vanilla extract. Reduce the heat and simmer for 20 minutes, stirring to keep the rice from sticking and burning; add a little water if the rice becomes too dry. The rice is cooked when it's soft and fluffy and there is no liquid in the pan, about 20 minutes.

Remove the rice from the heat and stir in the maple syrup. Serve at room temperature or chilled, drizzled with plenty of blackberry orange syrup.

SWEET TIP: Make extra syrup to drizzle over ice cream or swirl into a vodka cocktail.

MAPLE CHOCOLATE WHIP

Serves 6 to 8

Here's how to whip up elegance with ease—maple and dark chocolate make beautiful partners. The mellow sweetness of maple softens dark chocolate's deliciously bitter edge. Layer this into parfait glasses with nuts and chopped chocolate or fruit, or fill a baked tart shell or layer cake.

---

6 **ounces dark chocolate, 70 percent cacao or higher, chopped**
2 **teaspoons espresso powder**
¼ **cup maple syrup**
2 **cups heavy whipping cream, divided**

Melt the chocolate in a double boiler (a saucepan set over another saucepan filled one-quarter of the way with simmering water), stirring until the chocolate is silky and smooth. Stir in the espresso powder and maple syrup. Turn off the heat, but leave the saucepan in the water bath and stir in ¼ cup of the whipping cream to make a thick chocolate syrup. Remove and cool to room temperature.

In a medium bowl, whip the remaining cream to thick peaks. Fold the chocolate sauce into the whipped cream, leaving a few streaks. Turn the chocolate whip into a large serving bowl or individual glasses. Cover and refrigerate at least four hours before serving.

SWEET TIP: To vary the flavors, stir in ¼ cup chopped crystalized ginger, 1 teaspoon ground cardamom, or 1 teaspoon vanilla extract. Top with chopped nuts, fresh or dried berries, or shaved chocolate.

DANISH MARZIPAN HONEY-OAT TRUFFLES WITH RASPBERRIES

Makes about 20 to 25 candies

A traditional Danish Christmas treat, these require no baking and keep nicely for about a week. You'll want to use the best almond paste you can find, one with at least 45 percent almonds. Almond paste is available in most grocery stores, natural food co-ops, cooking shops, and online. Vary the candies by rolling them in freeze-dried fruit or shaved chocolate.

3⅓ tablespoons butter, softened to room temperature

1½ tablespoons honey

2 tablespoons cocoa powder

2 teaspoons cream

½ cup loosely packed, finely shredded almond paste

¾ cup quick-cooking oats

½ cup freeze-dried raspberries, crushed, for garnish

Line a baking sheet with parchment or wax paper. In a medium bowl, cream together the butter, honey, and cocoa powder, then work in the cream and almond paste. Work in oats a little at a time until fully incorporated. Using a teaspoon, measure out 20 to 25 one-teaspoon truffles, shaping them into balls with your fingers. If the dough is too sticky, lightly grease your hands with a little vegetable oil or softened butter. Line the truffles on the prepared baking sheet.

Put the crushed raspberries into a small bowl and then roll the truffles in the raspberries to coat. Store in an airtight container in the refrigerator or freeze if you need to store these for more than a week.

SWEET TIP: To vary the coating, substitute flaked coconut or chopped almonds for the crushed, freeze-dried raspberries.

Danish Marzipan Honey-Oat Truffles with Raspberries

MAPLE GINGER FRANGO

Serves 6 to 8

Make this beloved old-fashioned dessert ahead and keep in the freezer. Allow it to soften before serving with maple syrup and ground ginger.

---

1 **cup maple syrup, plus a little extra for garnish**

4 **eggs, separated**

¼ **cup finely chopped crystalized ginger**

2 **cups heavy cream**
  Dusting of ground ginger for garnish

In a medium-sized saucepan, warm the syrup, then whisk in egg yolks, one at a time. Bring the mixture to a simmer and cook over low heat, stirring constantly until it begins to thicken enough to coat the back of a spoon. Stir in the ginger and allow to cool. In a medium bowl, beat the egg whites until they hold soft peaks. In a separate bowl, whip the cream. Fold the egg whites and cream into the maple mixture; don't overmix (they should appear streaky). Pour the mixture into a 9-inch deep-dish pie pan or into individual serving goblets and put in the freezer until firm. Remove from the freezer and soften before serving with a drizzle of maple syrup and dusting of ground ginger.

SWEET TIP: The darker the maple syrup, the more pronounced the flavor of the frango will be.

MAPLE ESPRESSO MASCARPONE

Serves 6

Whip this up to fill store-bought meringue shells, chocolate cups, or a prebaked graham cracker or pastry crust, then garnish with fresh raspberries, strawberries, or sections of blood orange.

1½ **cups mascarpone**

¼ **cup maple syrup**

1 **to 2 tablespoons instant espresso powder**

In a small bowl, whisk all of the ingredients together. Serve in a meringue shell or pastry of your choice.

SWEET TIP: Try this spread over slices of toasted Maple Vanilla Half-Pound Cake (page 175).

MEYER LEMON CANNOLI

Serves 6

Meyer lemons are fragrant, thin-skinned, and less aggressive than most lemons—the perfect match to delicate ricotta. Use fresh sheep's milk ricotta if you are lucky enough to find it: it's slightly tangy and rich. Cow's milk ricotta also works well.

1½ **cups ricotta**

3 **tablespoons honey**

2 **tablespoons minced Meyer lemon, including the skin**

1 **teaspoon ground ginger**

6 **store-bought cannoli shells**

In a small bowl, whisk together ricotta, honey, lemon, and ginger. Using a small spoon, gently fill each cannoli with ¼ cup of the filling. It's easiest to fill from both ends. Serve immediately (the shells soften quickly).

SWEET TIP: Use a light, delicate honey here.

VERY BERRY GRANITA

Serves 6

Granita is a simple, very refreshing Italian dessert . . . a sophisticated version of shaved ice. Here the floral notes of honey accent the strawberries' natural fragrance. A food processor speeds up the work!

1 **pound fresh or frozen strawberries, hulled and sliced**

3 **tablespoons honey**

1 **teaspoon fresh lime juice**

   Generous pinch of salt

   A few grinds of black pepper for garnish

In a food processor fitted with a steel blade, puree all of the ingredients except the black pepper. Turn the mixture into a shallow baking dish or 8 x 8-inch pan and freeze, stirring occasionally. Just before serving, remove the pan, turn the frozen strawberry mix onto a cutting board, and chop into chunks. Working in batches, put the chunks into a food processor fitted with a steel blade and pulse until no large chunks remain. Serve garnished with a little coarsely ground pepper.

SWEET TIP: The black pepper gives the berries a nice hot kick, but try chopped fresh basil or mint to take the flavor in a different direction.

Strawberry Maple Trifle

STRAWBERRY MAPLE TRIFLE

Serves 4

This old-time elegant dessert makes a fine finish to a dinner party, but it's easy enough for a weeknight splurge. Use either fresh or frozen berries, but drain frozen berries well before adding to the mix. Use fresh berries when in season.

2   **10-ounce bags frozen strawberries**

¼   **cup port**

1   **tablespoon fresh orange juice**

6   **tablespoons maple syrup, divided**

1   **cup whipping cream**

12   **ladyfingers (savoiardi), broken into large pieces**

1   **to 2 tablespoons grated orange zest**

Coarsely chop the strawberries and place into a bowl. Once they have thawed slightly, stir in the port, orange juice, and 2 tablespoons of maple syrup.

Whip the cream to form soft peaks; set aside.

Spoon ¼ cup of the strawberry mixture into the bottom of 4 individual glasses or bowls, layer in half the whipped cream, half of the ladyfinger pieces, and repeat, topping off with the remaining strawberries. Sprinkle with orange zest. Drizzle the remaining maple syrup over each trifle. Cover and refrigerate for half an hour so the ladyfingers absorb all the flavors.

SWEET TIP: For a presentation worthy of a dinner party, layer the ingredients artfully in a glass serving bowl.

MOM'S FAVORITE MAPLE RUM RAISIN HAZELNUT ICE CREAM

Serves 6 to 8

Turn plain vanilla on its head with this easy addition of maple-sweetened nuts, raisins, good rum, and a little chopped chocolate.

½ cup golden raisins

¼ cup good-quality rum (e.g., Tattersall's blackstrap rum)

Vegetable oil for brushing baking sheet

⅓ cup maple sugar

1 tablespoon water

½ cup toasted, coarsely chopped hazelnuts (page 33)

2 to 3 ounces good dark chocolate, 75 to 85 percent cacao, coarsely chopped

1½ quarts vanilla ice cream

Maple syrup for drizzle

Soak the raisins in the rum in a small glass jar for at least 8 hours or overnight.

Line a small baking sheet with parchment paper and brush lightly with oil. In a small nonstick pan, melt together the maple sugar and water and stir in the chopped nuts. Turn the nut mixture out onto the parchment paper and spread with a spatula. Cool completely. Turn onto a cutting board and coarsely chop. Line one large or two smaller loaf pans with parchment paper.

Remove the ice cream from the freezer and allow it to soften slightly. Place ice cream in a large bowl. Stir the raisins, maple nuts, and chocolate into the ice cream. Pack the ice cream mixture into the prepared loaf pan(s) and cover with parchment paper. Return these to the freezer until firm.

To serve, warm the sides of the loaf pan with a hot towel. Upend the loaf pan onto a cutting board and remove the parchment; slice the ice cream loaf. Serve drizzled with a little maple syrup.

SWEET TIP: Offer Maple, Cornmeal, and Cranberry Biscotti (page 168) alongside the ice cream slices.

JAMMY COCONUT MINI TARTS

Makes 6 mini tarts

Dairy-free and 100 percent delicious, these tarts make a pretty last-minute dessert. Use Strawberry–Cranberry Ginger Orange Jam (page 36) or your favorite store-bought tart jam.

- 1 can (7.4 ounce) sweetened condensed coconut milk
- ½ cup Strawberry–Cranberry Ginger Orange Jam (page 36), or prepared strawberry jam
- 2 teaspoons lemon juice
- 1 tablespoon maple syrup
- 6 mini graham cracker pie crusts
- 2 tablespoons minced mint leaves, for garnish

In a small bowl, stir together the condensed coconut milk, jam, lemon juice, and maple syrup. Turn into the pie crusts and garnish with mint leaves. Chill for at least 30 minutes before serving to allow the flavors to blend.

SWEET TIP: You could also layer the filling with chopped nuts or crushed Italian almond cookies in individual parfait glasses.

LEMON-PISTACHIO PHYLLO CUPS

Makes 30 mini phyllo cups

These delicious phyllo bites are inspired by traditional Greek baklava. They are ultrasweet and rich—one bite will do you! You can bake these in a toaster oven.

2 packages mini phyllo cups, 30 total cups

¾ cup honey

½ cup water

1 tablespoon lemon zest

1 tablespoon lemon juice

½ teaspoon ground cinnamon

½ teaspoon ground cardamom

½ teaspoon ground fennel, optional

1 cup shelled pistachios, about 4½ ounces, chopped fine

Preheat the oven to 350°F. Line one or two cookie sheets with parchment paper and arrange the phyllo cups on the sheets.

In a small, heavy-bottomed saucepan, stir together honey, water, lemon zest and juice, cinnamon, cardamom, and fennel. Measure the depth using the dipstick method (page 69).

Set the pan over medium heat and bring the mixture to a gentle boil; reduce the heat and simmer, uncovered, until the syrup has reduced by half, about 10 to 15 minutes. Stir in the chopped pistachios and continue simmering, stirring occasionally, for another 2 minutes.

Remove the pan from heat and cool the mixture for a minute. Using a teaspoon, fill each of the cups with the nut mixture. Bake the cups until the filling is set, about 6 to 8 minutes. Remove and cool before serving. Store in an airtight container for up to a week.

SWEET TIP: Substitute almonds or walnuts for pistachios.

Lemon–Pistachio Phyllo Cups

GREEK HONEY LEMON RICOTTA PIE

Serves 10 to 12

This traditional Greek recipe for *melopita*, a custardy lemon pie, is delicious topped with fresh blueberries or dried cranberries, whose slight acidity helps balance the sweetness.

2 **eggs, lightly beaten**
½ **cup honey**
¼ **cup heavy cream**
Juice and zest of a Meyer lemon
Generous pinch of grated nutmeg
1 **blind-baked 9-inch Butter Pastry Dough (page 163)**

Preheat the oven to 350°F. In a large bowl, whisk together all of the ingredients (except the pastry crust). Spoon the filling over the pastry and bake until it's cooked through and a knife inserted in the center comes up clean, about 40 to 45 minutes. Remove and cool before serving.

SWEET TIP: To blind-bake, roll the crust out and fit into the pie or tart pan. Cut off a large square of parchment or aluminum foil to line the pan and snug the dough right up to the edges and sides of the pan. Pour pie weights or dried beans over the bottom of the dough (these weights will keep the crust from puffing up as it prebakes). Place the pie on a baking sheet and bake in a preheated 325°F oven until the edges of the crust are just beginning to turn golden, about 10 to 12 minutes. Remove. Grasp the corners of the parchment or foil and remove the weights (discard the beans if using them). The bottom of the pie will still look uncooked; return to the oven and continue baking another 3 to 5 minutes, cool, and then fill.

SWEET TIP: Make this with a mild honey, such as clover or basswood, that resembles the pale herb-scented honey of Greece.

DARK AND STORMY THREE-GINGER GINGERBREAD

Makes one 13 x 9-inch cake

The buckwheat honey makes this cake moist and dense, while fresh, crystalized, and ground ginger gives it plenty of punch. Serve with a splash of rum-spiked whipped cream or pair with sharp cheddar cheese and a full-bodied stout.

---

2 cups all-purpose flour

½ cup whole-wheat flour

1 tablespoon ground ginger

1½ teaspoons baking soda

½ teaspoon baking powder

½ teaspoon salt

¼ teaspoon ground black pepper

¼ cup buckwheat honey

1½ cups dark maple syrup

½ cup stout or water

¼ cup vegetable oil

2 tablespoons grated fresh ginger

½ cup (1 stick) butter, softened

2 large eggs

1 teaspoon finely grated orange zest

¼ cup chopped crystalized ginger

Preheat the oven to 350°F. Lightly grease and flour a 13 x 9-inch baking pan.

In a medium bowl, stir together the flours, ginger, baking soda, baking powder, salt, and black pepper. In a small bowl, stir together the honey, maple syrup, stout or water, and oil.

In a large bowl, using an electric mixer, cream together the grated fresh ginger and butter until light and fluffy and add the eggs one at a time, mixing well after each addition. Working in batches, stir this into the dry ingredients alternately with the honey mixture, until just combined. Fold in the orange zest and crystalized ginger. Pour the batter into the prepared pan. Bake until a toothpick inserted into the center of the cake comes out with only a few crumbs, about 45 minutes. Let the cake cool for an hour before serving.

SWEET TIP: Serve this plain or spread with Honey Cream Cheese Frosting (page 174).

HONEY WALNUT PIE

Makes one 9-inch pie

Superrich and sweet, this pie is best served in very thin slivers with just a dab of whipped cream.

Butter Pastry Dough for
a single-crust pie
(next page)

½ cup butter, melted

1½ cups honey

1 teaspoon vanilla extract

½ teaspoon salt

2 teaspoons orange zest

3 large eggs,
lightly beaten

1 heaping cup toasted,
chopped walnuts
(page 20)

Preheat the oven to 325°F. On a well-floured surface, roll the dough into a 13-inch circle and fit into the pie plate. Prick the bottom of the crust and bake until the edges just begin to brown, about 12 minutes. Remove and set aside.

In a medium bowl, whisk together butter, honey, vanilla extract, salt, and orange zest. Stir in the eggs, then the walnuts. Pour into the prepared pie pan. Bake until the filling is set and the walnuts smell toasty, about 35 minutes.

Honey and Cheese

In lieu of dessert, try these different pairings for an elegant after-dinner cheese plate with a sliced baguette or plain crackers:

- Ricotta drizzled with a mild floral basswood honey

- Triple crème Brie with dark, wildflower honey and toasted nuts

- Bold blue or Gorgonzola cheese with a strong dark honey such as honeydew or dandelion

- Parmigiano-Reggiano or aged cheddar cheese with savory marsh flower or sweet clover

BUTTER PASTRY DOUGH

Makes two 9- or 10-inch crusts

A simple crust, rich with butter for flavor and flakiness.

2½ **cups unbleached**
   all-purpose flour
 1 **teaspoon salt**
 1 **cup unsalted butter**
¼ **to ½ cup ice water**
 1 **teaspoon honey**

In a large bowl, whisk together the flour and salt. Dice the butter into small cubes. Work the butter into the flour using two knives or your fingers until pea-sized pieces of butter are scattered throughout the mixture.

Tossing with a fork, drizzle in the ice water and honey until the dough starts to come together and grabs your fingers. Gather the dough into a ball and divide it in half. Gently pat the shape of each half into a rough disk. Roll one disk out and cut to fit the pie pan. Wrap additional disk in plastic and store in the refrigerator or freeze for later use.

SWEET TIP: In a pinch? Use a prepared frozen pie shell but thaw and bake according to the recipe before adding the filling.

Very Chocolate Maple Brownies

VERY CHOCOLATE MAPLE BROWNIES

Makes 3 dozen brownies (easily doubled)

Fudgy and dark, these brownies are intensely rich—they are a terrific indulgence. They come together in no time flat.

---

2 **cups maple sugar**
1 **cup unsalted butter**
1 **tablespoon maple syrup**
4 **eggs**
10 **ounces bittersweet or unsweetened chocolate**
2 **teaspoons vanilla**
1½ **cups all-purpose flour**
½ **teaspoon salt**
Powdered sugar for garnish

Preheat the oven to 350°F. Line a 9 x 13-inch baking pan with parchment or generously grease with vegetable oil.

With an electric beater, cream together the maple sugar, butter, and maple syrup and then beat on high for at least 5 minutes. Then beat in the eggs one at a time.

Carefully melt the chocolate in a double boiler set over low heat or in the microwave, being careful not to scorch, until smooth.

Stir the melted chocolate into the butter mixture, then stir in the flour and salt and beat on medium for about 5 minutes. Turn into the prepared pan; smooth the top. Bake until a toothpick inserted into the center of the pan comes out clean, about 40 to 45 minutes. Garnish with the powdered sugar and cool on a wire rack before cutting.

SWEET TIP: If the maple sugar seems too coarse, grind it to become fine in a food processor fitted with a steel blade or a spice grinder.

HALVAH

Serves 8

One of the most common desserts in the world, halvah dates back to the Byzantine era some two thousand years ago. The soft, fudge-like candy, made from sesame paste, is extremely easy to make. A candy thermometer helps.

2 **cups honey**

1½ **cups tahini, stirred well**

2 **cups sliced almonds**

Generously grease a 2-cup loaf pan or cake pan with a removable bottom. Heat the honey over medium until a candy thermometer reaches 240°F or indicates the "soft ball" stage. To confirm, drop a bit of honey into a cup of cold water: it should form a sticky and soft ball that flattens when removed from the water.

In a separate pot, heat the tahini to 120°F. Add the warmed tahini to the honey and mix with a wooden spoon until it's smooth. Add the nuts and continue stirring until the mixture stiffens, about 6 to 8 minutes. Pour this into the prepared pan. Cool to room temperature. Wrap tightly with plastic wrap and place in the refrigerator for up to 36 hours to allow the sugar crystals to form and give the halvah its distinctive texture. Invert to remove from the pan; cut into pieces with a sharp knife. This will keep in the refrigerator tightly wrapped in plastic.

SWEET TIP: Drizzle with melted dark chocolate for a superrich treat.

PEANUT BUTTER CHOCOLATE CHUNK COOKIES

Makes about 2 dozen cookies

Just seven ingredients . . . and these are gluten-free! Use a natural peanut butter, but not one you ground yourself. These tend to make a very dry, crumbly cookie.

1½ **cups all-natural peanut butter, no sugar**

½ **cup honey**

2 **teaspoons vanilla**

2 **eggs, lightly beaten**

½ **teaspoon baking soda**
    Pinch of salt

¼ **cup chopped dark or milk chocolate**

¼ **cup toasted peanuts, optional**

Preheat the oven to 350°F. Line a baking sheet with parchment paper. In a large bowl, cream together the peanut butter and honey. Beat in the vanilla, eggs, baking soda, and salt. Gently fold in the chocolate and peanuts, if using.

Using a teaspoon, drop the cookies onto a cookie sheet about 2 inches apart and gently press with your fingers to flatten into circles. Bake until the cookies have just started to brown and the edges look firm, about 8 to 10 minutes. Remove and cool on the cookie sheet for about 5 minutes; then transfer to a wire rack to cool completely.

SWEET TIP: Some peanut butters are saltier than others, so taste before you make the cookies and adjust the amount of salt accordingly.

MAPLE, CORNMEAL, AND CRANBERRY BISCOTTI

Makes about 1 dozen biscotti

These pretty, golden biscotti, sparked with dried cranberries, are not too sweet and pack a lovely, corny crunch. Ideal for dunking in morning coffee and afternoon tea!

¾ cups all-purpose flour

¼ cup coarse, stone-ground cornmeal

½ cup maple sugar

½ teaspoon baking soda

⅛ teaspoon salt

1 large egg, beaten

1 teaspoon vanilla extract

1 tablespoon orange zest

2 tablespoons butter, melted

½ cup dried cranberries

Preheat the oven to 350°F. Line a baking sheet with parchment paper.

In a large bowl, whisk together the flour, cornmeal, maple sugar, baking soda, and salt. In a separate bowl, whisk together the egg, vanilla extract, and orange zest. Make a well in the center of the flour mixture and pour in the beaten egg mixture. Stir in the butter and mix until the dough is wet and crumbly. Add the dried cranberries and mix well.

Turn the dough out onto a lightly floured counter and knead until smooth. Work the dough into a log that is about 3 inches wide and 7 inches long and transfer to the baking sheet. Bake until the log feels set, about 20 minutes. Remove from the oven and allow to cool for a few minutes. Reduce the oven heat to 250°F.

Using a sharp, serrated knife, slice the log crosswise into individual cookies and place on the baking sheet cut side down. Bake until lightly browned, about 5 to 8 minutes; remove from the oven, turn the slices over, and then continue baking until nicely browned, another 5 minutes. Cool on wire racks before storing in an airtight container.

SWEET TIP: For a crunchier biscotti, increase the baking time by 2 to 3 minutes per side.

Maple, Cornmeal, and Cranberry Biscotti

MARLA'S PERISHKAS

Makes about 3 dozen cookies

One wintry afternoon, I learned to make perishkas with Dr. Marla Spivak, Distinguished McKnight Professor in Entomology at the University of Minnesota. As a child, Marla made these holiday treats with her Russian Jewish grandmother, who never used a recipe but eyeballed quantities and baked by feel. Thank goodness Marla recorded the process with copious notes on sheets of paper (now crumpled and yellowed with age). As we measured, chopped, and kneaded in her sunny kitchen, Marla talked about her work with bees in the university's Bee Lab. Committed to promoting the conservation, health, and diversity of bee pollinators, the Bee Lab provides opportunities for research and academic study as well as hosting beekeeping classes for students of all levels and backgrounds.

These pastries have different names in different homes, and their ingredients vary from cook to cook. But they are always doused in honey to be finger-licking delicious, just right with a cup of strong coffee or a glass of port.

DOUGH

- 2 **medium oranges**
- ⅓ **cup sugar**
- 2 **eggs**
- 1 **cup melted butter**
- 3 **to 4 cups flour, plus more for kneading the dough**
- ½ **teaspoon baking powder**
- ½ **teaspoon baking soda**
- ½ **teaspoon salt**
- ¼ **cup poppy seeds**

Preheat the oven to 350°F.

Zest the oranges and squeeze the orange juice into a large bowl. You should have about ⅓ cup orange juice and 3 tablespoons zest. Beat in the sugar, eggs, and butter until light.

In a separate bowl, sift together 3 cups of flour, baking powder, baking soda, and salt. Stir the dry ingredients and the poppy seeds into the wet ingredients. If the dough is too wet, add a little more flour to create a soft dough. It should not be too stiff, so add only enough flour to knead it without being too sticky.

Turn the dough out onto a lightly floured board and knead it until it is soft and smooth.

In a separate bowl, stir together the filling ingredients.

Using a floured rolling pin, roll out the dough into a rectangle about ¼ inch thick. Cut the dough into strips that are approximately 2 to 3 inches wide by 8 to 10 inches long. Place a dollop of filling at one end of the strip, close to the top. Fold the top part of the strip over the filling, then fold the dough over itself in a triangle to seal in the filling. Cut the strip at the bottom of the

FILLING

½ **cup chopped walnuts**

½ **cup sweetened shredded coconut**

1 **cup plum, apricot, or sour cherry jam**

¼ **cup raisins**

DOUSING

1 **cup honey or more as needed**

Bourbon

triangle. Repeat this process with the rest of the strip. You will get between 5 to 8 small triangles for each strip.

Place the triangles on a lightly greased baking sheet. Repeat folding process with all of the dough.

Bake the cookies until lightly browned, about 15 to 20 minutes. Remove from the oven and set on a board or rack to cool.

Turn the honey into a small pot and set over medium heat; add about ¼ cup water and warm until the honey is thin. Drop the perishkas into the honey and gently turn them over in the honey. Remove the perishkas and place them, not more than two to three deep, in a shallow baking dish. Pour in a capful or so of bourbon, then light with a match. Repeat until the cookies have all been doused in the honey (you may need to add more honey) and flamed with bourbon.

SWEET TIP: You can make these in steps over a day or two. Prepare the dough and filling and store in the refrigerator. Bring to room temperature before you start working with them again.

Carrot Cake with Honey
Cream Cheese Frosting

CARROT CAKE WITH HONEY CREAM CHEESE FROSTING

Serves 14 to 18

Honey enhances the earthy sweetness of carrots and makes for a dense, moist cake. Serve this flavorful cake unadorned or gild it with cream cheese frosting—or simply drizzle with honey and top with chopped nuts.

1¾ cups all-purpose flour

2 teaspoons baking powder

1 teaspoon baking soda

2 teaspoons ground cinnamon

1 teaspoon ground nutmeg

½ teaspoon ground cloves

½ teaspoon salt

½ cup honey

¾ cup coconut oil, softened

3 large eggs

1 tablespoon vanilla extract

4 large carrots, shredded, about 2⅔ cups

Honey Cream Cheese Frosting (next page)

Preheat the oven to 350°F. Line a 13 x 9-inch cake pan with parchment paper.

In a medium bowl, whisk together the flour, baking powder, baking soda, cinnamon, nutmeg, cloves, and salt. In a large bowl, whisk together the honey, oil, eggs, and vanilla. Stir in the carrots. Add the flour mixture and fold together with a rubber spatula until just combined.

Pour the batter into the prepared pan and smooth the top. Bake the cake until it is set and firm to the touch, about 20 to 25 minutes. Remove from the oven and allow the cake to cool in the pan for about 20 minutes. Remove the cake from the pan and spread frosting evenly over the top and sides.

SWEET TIP: You can make this as a layer cake by baking the batter in two 8-inch round or square pans.

(continued on next page)

HONEY CREAM CHEESE FROSTING

Makes 3 cups

If you have more icing than you need for the cake, store it in a covered container in the refrigerator for up to one week. It's perfect on toasted bagels or on French toast. Do not use low-fat cream cheese or the resulting frosting will be soupy.

12 **ounces cream cheese, softened**

½ **cup (1 stick) unsalted butter, softened**

2 **teaspoons vanilla extract**

6 **tablespoons honey**
   Generous pinch of salt

In a medium bowl, whip together the cream cheese, butter, vanilla, honey, and salt to taste.

MAPLE VANILLA HALF-POUND CAKE

Makes one 9 x 3-inch loaf cake

This loaf is inspired by old-fashioned recipes for pound cake, though we cut the quantities in half. It's finished with a vanilla–bourbon maple glaze.

2 cups unbleached all-purpose flour
¾ teaspoon baking powder
¼ teaspoon salt
1 cup (2 sticks) unsalted butter, softened
1 cup maple sugar
2 teaspoons vanilla
4 eggs, well beaten

GLAZE
½ cup maple syrup
2 tablespoons bourbon
1 vanilla bean, split, or 2 teaspoons vanilla extract

Lightly grease and flour a 9 x 3-inch loaf pan. Preheat the oven to 325°F.

In a large bowl, stir together the flour, baking powder, and salt. In a separate bowl, cream the butter until light and fluffy; beat in the sugar, then the vanilla and eggs. The mixture will look separated. Fold in the dry ingredients, quickly and gently. The batter will be thick. Pour the batter into the prepared pan and bake until a toothpick inserted in the center comes up clean, about 1 hour. Cool in the pan for about 10 minutes, then remove and cool completely on a wire rack before drizzling with the glaze.

Glaze: In a small saucepan, stir together all of the ingredients and set over medium heat and bring to a simmer. Simmer for about 30 seconds; remove from heat. Remove the vanilla bean if using and discard.

SWEET TIP: If the maple sugar seems coarse, grind it in a clean spice or coffee grinder until it is as fine as regular white sugar. Or you may choose to use coarse maple sugar, which will give the cake a sandy texture that is very pleasant.